The Zen of Groups

A Handbook for People Meeting with a Purpose

Dale Hunter □ Anne Bailey □ Bill Taylor

FISHER
BOOKS™

Publishers: Howard Fisher
Helen V. Fisher

North American Howard Fisher
Editors: Sarah Smith

Cover Design: Josh Young

Book Design: Edgar H. Allard

Book Production: Deanie Wood

North American Edition
Published by Fisher Books, LLC
5225 W. Massingale Road
Tucson, AZ 85743-8416
(520) 744-6110
www.fisherbooks.com

Originally published in 1992
by Tandem Press, Auckland

© 1995 Fisher Books
Printed in USA
Printing 10 9 8 7 6

**Library of Congress
Cataloging-in-Publication Data**

Hunter, Dale, 1943-
  The Zen of groups: a handbook for people meeting with a
purpose / Dale Hunter,
Anne Bailey, Bill Taylor.
    p. cm.
  Includes bibliographical
references and index.
  ISBN 1-55561-100-1
  1. Communication in small
groups. 2. Decision-making,
Group. 3. Work groups. 4. Social
facilitation. 5. Conflict management. I. Bailey, Anne, 1944- .
II. Taylor, Bill, 1942- . III. Title.
HM133.H88 1995
302.3'4--dc20   95-31932
                              CIP

Notice: The information in this book is true and complete to the best of our knowledge. It is offered with no guarantees on the part of the authors or Fisher Books. The authors and publisher disclaim all liability in connection with use of this book. Fisher Books are available at special quantity discounts for educational use. Special books or book excerpts can also be created to fit specific needs. For details please write or telephone.

Welcome

Welcome to the Zen of Groups.

We acknowledge you, the reader,
for sharing this book with us.

We acknowledge the richness of group life we
have experienced with its many cultural strands.

We acknowledge the opportunities we have had
to work with a great variety of organizational,
community, family, educational and support
groups.

We acknowledge our friends, colleagues and
families for their love and encouragement.

We acknowledge our own commitment to
contribute our experience to others.

We acknowledge the higher purpose of
this book which is to contribute to creating
synergy on the planet.

From our hearts to your heart—enjoy.

Zen

Zen has been described as the inner art and design of the Orient. It was taken from India to China in the sixth century and probably dates back to before Buddhism and Christianity. It has been described as a special teaching without scriptures, beyond words and letters, pointing to the mind-essence of humanity, seeing directly into one's nature, attaining enlightenment. Zen points us towards observing the flowering of our human nature through moment-by-moment consciousness, and our passing through life as a petal falling from a flower.

Zen has been passed down from master to student through direct heart-to-heart experience, with the student always living and meditating close to the master. The Zen practice of being fully awake and in action moment by moment is the essence of group synergy and has inspired us in writing this book.

Fragments of Zen wisdom are to be found in many stories describing self-discoveries of Zen masters and students. Here is one story which illustrates the irony of our writing a book as a way of passing on our experiences of group development.

What Are You Doing?
What Are You Saying?

The Zen master Mu-nan had only one successor. His name was Shoju. After Shoju had completed the study of Zen, Mu-nan called him into his room.

"I am getting old," Mu-nan said, "and you are the only one who will carry on my teaching. As my successor, I am giving you a valuable book. It has been passed down from master to master for seven generations. I also have added many points according to my understanding."

"If the book is such an important thing, you had better keep it," Shoju replied. "I received your Zen without writing and am satisfied with it as it is."

"I know that," said Mu-nan. "Even so, this work has been carried from master to master for seven generations, so you may keep it as a symbol of receiving the teaching. Here it is."

The two happened to be talking in front of a fire. The instant Shoju felt the book in his hands he threw it into the flames. He had no desire for possessions.

Mu-nan, who had never been angry before, yelled, "What are you doing?"

Shoju shouted back, "What are you saying?"

Contents

Introduction

The purpose of this book

We all belong to groups all our lives. Making the most of being in groups is a valuable life skill. This book comes out of a belief that the effectiveness of all groups can be vastly increased.

The purpose of the book is to alter consciousness about what is possible for groups and to provide access to group synergy. It offers insight into what makes groups work powerfully. It includes a large selection of exercises and techniques to assist your group to move through the processes and stages which will make this possible.

The book is designed to appeal to a broad spectrum of readers involved in organizations, business, community groups, education and recreation. It is written to be accessible to everyone who is part of a work, community, social, family or support group. And it will be useful for all the groups you are in, particularly those of up to 30 people.

The leadership role we explore in depth is that of a facilitator.

How to use this book

This book is designed to be read slowly and thoughtfully. Look for what rings true for you and use your own experience with groups to see what could happen to take those groups you are in to the next stage of development.

We want to challenge your ideas about what can happen in groups, and you can participate in this by taking time to consider the questions under the headings *Thinking Points*. There are no right answers to these questions—the value is in the process of inquiring. You may like to jot down your own responses to help with your process. The first nine chapters contain the essence of effective work in groups. These are followed by a toolkit of techniques and exercises (tools).

Learning about groups is a bit like learning a new language. Your progress may be slow at times, but then something will drop into place and a whole new area will open up.

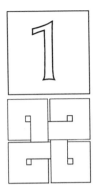

The Nature of Groups

We're talking about us

The first thing to know about people in groups is that we are talking about us—ordinary humans like our family members, friends and coworkers, and ourselves. This is important to get established right at the beginning.

This book is about the actual experience of being in a group as an active member, not about observing groups from the outside looking in. This book is for those who are already getting their feet wet or their socks dirty—that is, people who are part of a group which is up to something. It's about you being more effective in the groups you are part of.

Most of us are not trained to operate successfully in groups and our inability to be effective is often frustrating and confusing.

A group of individuals

A group is made up of individuals. You, as an individual person, are different. And you have your own:

Family	Friends
Networks	Culture
Fellow workers	Other groups
Lovers	Associations and allegiances
Community	Town/city
Nation	Place in the world

Out of this background come your own particular:

Ideas	Beliefs
Hang-ups	Desires
Tragedies	Sense of humor
Level of tolerance towards others	Level of tolerance towards yourself
Memories	Hopes and fears
Dreams	Internal dialogue
Ways of speaking	Patterns of behavior

You, as a group member, come to a group with all of the above. We can describe this as *baggage*. Baggage is not right or wrong, it just is. We all have it. It helps to be familiar with your own baggage and to know what is contained in the various *suitcases*.

Given everything you take into a group, it is not surprising that being part of one is often a challenging experience loaded with possibilities and pitfalls.

Thinking Points _____

➠ Am I aware of some of my baggage?
➠ Am I comfortable with my baggage?
➠ Do I allow room for the baggage of others?

Who needs a group?

A camel is a horse designed by a committee!

People have a mixed attitude towards groups. On the one hand, you probably belong to all sorts of work, social, community and sporting groups. On the other hand, you will often be unhappy with group processes:

Groups take too long.
I'd rather do it myself.
It's too frustrating to be part of a group.

So, why should you be part of a group? When you want to do something you cannot achieve on your own, a group can be the most effective way to get it done. *But if you can do it alone, you don't need a group.*

What kinds of groups are there?

Some kinds of groups are:

Nuclear family	Extended family
Households	Support groups
Project groups	Work groups
Task teams	Sports groups
Cultural groups	Hobbies groups
Special-interest groups	Classes

There are also many other kinds of groups.

This book is mainly for groups of up to 30 people. Larger groups need different structures and processes. We will discuss these in Chapter 9.

Who belongs to the group?

Some groups have clearly identified members—you are part of the group or not part of the group and everyone clearly understands who is in it. Family and work groups are usually like this. Some groups are open and people can join and leave any time they want to.

It is not so easy to develop group identity when people are joining and leaving all the time. You may feel uncomfortable if someone joins your group without consultation or prior agreement by the whole group. This can also happen if someone leaves your group without saying anything or if they miss a session with no explanation.

It is helpful for your group to discuss the issue of membership at the first meeting. Clarifying this at an early stage can avoid confusion and conflict later on. Some of the membership choices which need to be made are:

- ☐ Is membership to be open (anyone can come to any meeting) or closed (only agreed people may attend)?
- ☐ Is what is discussed to be kept private?
- ☐ Do you all need to attend every meeting?
- ☐ What procedure do you and others follow if you can't attend?
- ☐ Can you bring guests with or without prior agreement?

If your group wants its work, decisions, or personal sharing to be confidential, then clear rules for membership are very important. Also, see Ground rules, Chapter 4, page 28.

Choosing a group

Apart from your family, most groups are groups you *choose* to belong to. When you are thinking about joining a new group, it helps to think about the following issues

- ☐ What is the purpose of the group?
- ☐ Is this important to me?
- ☐ Is there a group which will suit me better?
- ☐ When and for how long does the group meet?
- ☐ What else will be involved in my being a part of the group?
- ☐ Extra time? Money? Tasks?

Some groups require more time and commitment than others. A nuclear family is a group requiring large amounts of time and high commitment. A hobbies group may require less time and be a low-commitment group.

What's special about a group?

One + One + One + One = Five

Something special can happen in a group of people who are working together towards a common objective. This something special is called *synergy*.

Synergy = the combined effect of parts that exceeds their individual effects

You have probably experienced group synergy at some time when your group is operating well—the energy is high and things take off. You achieve more than you thought possible.

In this book we explore synergy—what it is, what creates it, what maintains it and what recreates it. This book is about synergy in groups and how you can enable your group to access synergy.

➠ Consider the energy available to a mother who lifts a car off a trapped child.

➠ Consider the energy between two people passionately in love.

➠ What if this energy is available to any group that you are part of?

➠ What then becomes possible within your family and in your work, play, in your community and the world?

➠ Rules, formulas and processes are useful as guidelines in the same way that a map through the mountains can assist you to avoid some of the dangers of difficult terrain.

Synergy in groups is about you and everyone else being present to yourselves and to the other group members, and acting moment by moment in a kind of verbal dance which guides your group towards fulfilling its purpose.

This is the Zen of Groups

We are not saying it is easy to create group synergy or that it happens without working on it. Rather, it is like training a herd of wild horses and developing them into a successful team.

A group includes each individual with all his or her baggage. Operating synergistically means working together without tripping over your own or other people's baggage.

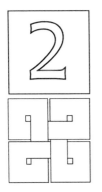

2 Group Issues

This chapter covers three key issues which must be recognized in your group for it to be effective and begin to develop synergy. These are leadership, power relationships and the neglected area of feelings. Each needs to be taken care of if your group is to develop trust and group identity.

Leadership

Leadership is about providing focus, direction and inspiration in a group. Leaders enable a group to imagine and create a future which will fulfill the group purpose. As a leader, you will do this mostly by speaking in a way that encourages or inspires your group members to take action. An effective leader gives power to (empowers) other group members.

Leadership is a natural function of people working together in groups. Leadership comes out of a group. There are no leaders without groups, although there are sometimes groups without leadership. Leaders are recognized in a group by the group members:

You are the leader.
We recognize that you are providing us with leadership.

Leadership is *fluid*. Leaders change over time and also with different situations.

A group often has a different leader for each aspect of the group project. A sports team may have different leaders on and off the field. A work group may have a different leader for each part of a project.

Leadership is not personal. You probably belong to many groups and may provide leadership in some and not in others.

- ☐ Anne is a leader of several groups. She is a member of a professional support group.
- ☐ Dale coaches team leaders of project groups She also leads some project groups.
- ☐ Bill is a member of a drumming group. The group leader is his drum teacher. Others lead the group when the teacher is not present. Bill has organized some of the group's functions.

A leader can lead only with the consent (spoken or unspoken) of group members. If a leader has consent from some group members but not others, you will have a divided group or a faction. If the consent of the group has not been given or has been given and then withdrawn, a person is not the group leader.

Often a group wants to formalize the leadership role. This can be done by choosing a group member to formally take on the role of *leader*. A name may be used such as *group* or *project leader, facilitator, spokesperson* or *team captain*.

It is useful to be aware of the difference between leadership as a natural part of groups and the formal role of group leader. Formal leaders need to develop an understanding of leadership so they can inspire and provide direction to groups consciously, and not only when they are feeling enthusiastic. The formal leader also needs to recognize and encourage leadership within the group and suggest ways in which leaders can be developed. A previous leader may become mentor to a new leader.

☐ Bob was the president of a professional organization. Now he is the past president and supports the new president by advising him on resources and strategy.

Thinking Points_____

➠ In what groups do you play a leadership role?
➠ In what circumstances are you likely to be a leader?
➠ Who do you recognize as leaders in the groups you are in?
➠ Are they the formal leaders?
➠ When did each group last choose or change a leader?
➠ As a leader how can you empower others?

The leadership role we will explore in depth is that of facilitator.

*A facilitator's job is to make it easy for a group
to be successful.
Facilitate = to make easy or more convenient.*

A facilitator guides the group through or past pitfalls and danger and towards the enabling and empowering pathways which will allow for synergistic action to show up.

In a fully effective group, each person may have the skills and experience to facilitate the group and the role may be rotated.

In practice, the skills associated with group facilitation are not well developed or known and a facilitator may be a particular person in the group who has the skills.

An outside facilitator can also be brought in by the group to carry out this role. Guidelines for a facilitator are presented in Chapter 6. See also Tool 60.

Power

Being part of a group is not necessarily a happy or comfortable experience for many people. One of the reasons for this has to do with issues relating to power.

Some people are able to speak out, assert and express themselves in a group. Other people feel shy about talking, taking part in discussions and expressing themselves in front of others. Some people readily initiate discussion while others tend to respond or react to others' ideas and suggestions. Each of us is different, with our own behavior patterns.

We all have ideas and beliefs about power and its use, and we bring these ideas and beliefs to our group. Some people believe that power is of itself a bad thing. A common saying is that *Power corrupts and absolute power corrupts absolutely.* But power is not bad. It is neutral. Power can be used or misused. The more you know about power and how it works, the more you will be able to use it effectively to empower the group.

There are different kinds of power in a group:

Positional power   Personal power
Assigned power   Factional power
Knowledge power

Positional power is when a person in the group has a more powerful position than other group members in the organization or community of which the group is a part. This person may be a manager, an elected representative, city council member, teacher or other important person. People with positional power will usually have more power in the group than other individuals. They will be listened to more carefully and their opinions given more weight. Positional power is given outside the group and recognized within the group. Positional power may include the ability to override group decisions through intervening outside the group.

Assigned power is when the group assigns a particular role to a group member which allows that person more power. Such a role could be as group or project leader, facilitator, record keeper, financial controller, spokesperson for the group or team captain. Assigned power is given by the group and withdrawn by the group.

Knowledge power is when a group member has specialist knowledge and experience in an area related to the work of the group. The person may be a computer whiz, accountant, urban planner, medical professional, expert in a language or culture—and so on. Knowledge and experience need to be relevant to the group. Often knowledge power is held by group members who already have positional or assigned power.

Personal power is when a person, through personal skills and qualities, is looked to as a guide or leader by group members. He or she may have skills in communication or have special style or charisma related to his or her life experience. This person may not have a position of assigned power within the group or any positional power. Other factors which can influence personal power in a group include age, sex, ethnic background, marital status, length of involvement or physical appearance.

Factional power is when several people within a group act together in an organized way to influence or dominate group process or decision-making. The degree to which a faction is powerful in a group may depend on the number of people involved, whether they also have positional or other kinds of power, and whether or not they form a majority.

Power is always a factor in every group and it will be useful for you to identify and be aware of how power is expressed. Recurring conflict in a group is often the result of unclear or unrecognized power relationships. Group members can become skilled at recognizing, clarifying and working through power issues. The power relationships of a group can become conscious or spoken through group exercises. See Tool 61.

For a group to be effective and synergistic each individual in the group needs to feel comfortable and able to express themselves, and be recognized by the other members of the group as a full participant. *A group is as effective as its weakest member.* This is a useful guide to use when you are analyzing and clarifying power issues.

Thinking Points

➠ Who has the least power in your group and why?
➠ What do they have to say about it?
➠ Who has the different kinds of power in your group?
➠ What do they have to say about it?
➠ Are there ways that power can be more evenly shared within the group?
➠ Would this enhance or detract from the effectiveness of the group?

Feelings

Leadership and power are usually recognized as playing an important role in the functioning of a group. What is often overlooked or ignored is the importance and power of feelings. Because they are not *rational,* the traditional business world has often failed to recognize the key role of feelings in human interaction. The result is unbalanced and dysfunctional ways of working which lead to stress, alienation and illness in the workplace.

We all have feelings. We all have feelings about ourselves, others and every aspect of life. We live in a sea of feelings. We experience feelings minute by minute and they range in intensity and variety. Some people are more aware of their feelings than others.

Some people experience life as if they are totally at the mercy of their feelings. Feelings occur automatically when something happens. It is like the weather when a storm is approaching—you don't seem to have any control over it. The feeling hits and you immediately *become* that feeling and express it whether you want to or not. You *are* that feeling.

We often refer to our feelings as *good* or *bad.* Feelings are really not good or bad, but they can have us feeling uncomfortable and vulnerable.

Each person in your group is likely to be experiencing a feeling most of the time. Here is a list of some of the ways we feel:

Happy	Sad	Excited
Nervous	Bored	Angry
Pleased	Frightened	Exhilarated
Comfortable	Worried	Disappointed
Expectant	Nurtured	Energized
Unsure	Delighted	Amused

The important thing is to experience or *have* feelings rather than be *had by* or be at the mercy of them, and to be able to *choose* whether or where you express them.

Naming your feelings is the first step to having some power and ease with them. If this is difficult for you it may be useful to have some individual sessions with a counselor who can assist you to separate yourself a little from your sea of feelings. It is a bit like learning to swim.

When you are part of a group you need to be aware of your own and other members' feelings. There are three types of feelings you need to be aware of:

1. Old feelings

These are feelings you carry as part of your baggage—stuck feelings from the past that you get tripped up by. They *go off* like explosions when you are triggered, perhaps by a certain word. Someone may say *father, marriage, child* and you immediately flash back to a past experience and all the feelings associated with it. You may have particular traumatic experiences (say the unresolved death of a husband or child with all its associated grief) which you are often triggered back to. Old feelings also include recurrent feelings of longing or worry about the future.

2. Present-time feelings

These come up in the present and are spontaneous and fluid. They come and go like waves and usually don't last long. They generally fall into one of four categories—*love, fear, anger* or *grief*—with lots of variations and intensities. If a feeling hangs around, it is likely you have been triggered into an old feeling.

3. Group feelings

These are present-time feelings which are shared by the group: The whole group is excited, sad, enthusiastic or disappointed. Group feelings are important as they are part of the development of trust and group identity.

Group exercises to clarify and express feelings are given in Tools 46-48. It is useful for your group to practice some of these and get to be comfortable talking about and naming feelings.

Thinking Points _____

➡ Do I have feelings or do they have me?
➡ Which of my feelings hang around the longest?
➡ What experiences do they remind me of from the past?
➡ What feelings do I express spontaneously?
➡ What group feelings have I seen expressed in the group?
➡ Did they help to unify the group?

Developing trust and group identity

For a group to become effective, it is necessary for members to feel a part of it. Recognizing and attending to leadership, power relationships and feelings will provide a base on which trust can develop. It takes time for group identity to develop and for members to feel they belong.

As members take care of these issues and begin to share and recognize common experiences, beliefs and values, they begin to warm to one another and establish links which build relation-ship, bonding and trust. We trust people we understand or relate to. The quicker group members discover these links, the quicker group bonding and identity can develop.

Then, as group members begin to feel safe, take risks, try new things, and express themselves, a group identity begins to develop. The group becomes *our* group. Group members *belong* to the group and are proud of *their* group. They *stick up for it* and have a sense of commitment to it. This development of group identity is necessary before synergy can occur.

To speed up the process of developing group identity, use Tools 38-45.

How Groups Work

Stages in the life of a group

Groups have a *life cycle*. Like a person, a group goes through a number of different stages before reaching full potential and maturity. The stages of a group may not be quite as obvious as for an individual. Here is a way of describing these stages.

1. Getting Started

Birth Stage: This stage starts with the idea of forming a group and goes through the enrollment of group members, preparation and holding the first meeting, agreement on purpose, agenda and initial processes. Group members are likely to feel anticipation, excitement, nervousness or shyness.

2. Getting Comfortable

Early Childhood Stage: Group members get to know one another, remind one another of common friends, family and co-workers, and establish areas of similarity in beliefs and values, hopes, fears and experiences. The group is likely to establish group roles (facilitator, recorder) at this stage. Group members begin to feel warmth and friendship towards one another as well as acceptance and growing trust.

3. Getting to Work

Schooldays Stage: This is the stage where the group begins to get down to work, allocates tasks, and group members make commitments. In a support group the sharing and trust deepens. Group members feel willing and keen to contribute and establish their presence. Some may begin to experience irritation with the pace of the group (too fast or slow) and with other participants, such as:

> *Donald is beginning to annoy me. Imagine Rita saying that!*
> Usually these comments will be made to other participants outside the group meeting.

4. Getting to be Right

Teenage Adjustment Stage: This is the stage when differences emerge, challenges are made, conflicts arise, are worked through or left to fester. And people either honor or don't honor their commitments. Personalities have now become more defined, alliances and factions formed and *positions* taken. Limits on tasks may be set, purpose and processes may be redefined. Some group members may feel frustrated, angry, repressed, overworked, unappreciated, unhappy, or turned off. Other group members may feel powerful and that they are *winning* or getting their point across. A group member may leave the group, or wish he could leave. Here is an example:

> A project group is in the sixth month of a 12-month project. The project is not going as well as expected. The

group members are all very competent people and have strong personalities.

Anne seems to be irritable a lot of time, especially with Bill. Bill is relaxed, but does not seem fully committed to, or extended by the project. Dale is also involved in another project and seems to have lots of reasons for not meeting deadlines. Bob, the team leader, is under pressure from his manager to produce results from this project. He is feeling resentful and unappreciated by the team members.

The project group has a series of heated meetings where there is a lot of shouting and blaming. Dale storms out of a meeting, threatening to ask to be transferred off of the project. All group members are feeling resentful and are complaining about one another to others.

5. Getting to Synergy

Maturity Stage: Group members recommit to the group purpose at a deeper level, recognizing that the group is more than the individual personalities with all their foibles.

Group members allow room for their own and others' baggage and take responsibility for their own response when something happens in the group to upset or distract them (when they get *triggered* or *tripped up*). They stop blaming each other. The group establishes ways to strengthen group identity, acknowledges successes, accepts differences and resolves conflicts. The group clarifies specific outcomes which will be achieved in stated time frames. Support systems are set up to ensure success. Group members feel empowered, excited and a strong sense of belonging. See also Chapter 7, Synergy.

6. Ending

Fulfillment and Completion Stage: The group purpose is fulfilled and the tasks completed. In some cases the purpose may not have been fulfilled but circumstances have altered and the group has ended anyway. The support group has completed the agreed sessions and decided not to continue. The group may hold an evaluation session to assess its effectiveness and draw out the learning. Group members acknowledge their own and others' contribution. Members feel satisfied or dissatisfied, complete or not complete. They will often be nostalgic, emotional or may not want the group to end. Some members may feel relieved. A project group may choose to begin a new project.

Note:

Withdrawal Stage: Most groups do not move from Stage 4 (Teenage Adjustment Stage) to Stage 5 (Maturity Stage). They either stay in Stage 4 or lapse into a Withdrawal Stage.

Group members settle for *This is as good as it gets* or *This is the way life is.* Group members find working together a struggle or boring, but keep going anyway. The fun has gone out of working together. They lose faith in the project and one another. Privately, group members feel compromised, sad and unheard. They stop challenging one another and just do what they have to do. They begin to daydream about a better project or group that they will be part of in the future.

Thinking Points _____

➡ What stage is your group at?
➡ How long has it been at this stage?
➡ What is needed to move to the next stage?
➡ Has the group reached Getting to Synergy yet?
➡ How can the group maintain the Getting to Synergy stage?

Roles

A lot of work has been done by researchers on identifying the roles people play in groups. Identification of roles can raise the awareness of your groups and assist in identifying patterns of behavior and habits of interaction which members may be adopting without knowing.

Here are some commonly recognized roles:

Task Roles

Initiator—brings new ideas or new approaches.

Opinion-giver—provides pertinent beliefs about what the group is considering.

Elaborator—builds on suggestions from others.

Clarifier—gives relevant examples, restates the problem, and probes for meaning and understanding.

Process Roles

Tension-reliever—uses humor or suggests breaks.

Compromiser—is willing to yield a point of view.

Harmonizer—mediates/reconciles.

Encourager—uses praise and support.

Gate-keeper—keeps communication open and encourages others.

Blocking Roles

Aggressor—deflates others' status or disagrees aggressively.

Negator—criticizes or attacks others.

Blocker—holds on to attitudes, mentions unrelated experiences or returns to already resolved topics.

Withdrawer—will not participate. May have private conversations or take notes.

Recognition-seeker—boasts or talks excessively.
Topic-jumper—changes the subject.
Joker—diffuses the energy by telling jokes.
Devil's advocate—presents the other point of view.
This role can be positive.

Thinking Points _____

➨ Do you recognize yourself and others in any of these roles?
➨ Do you play a number of roles?
➨ Are these in the same or different groups?
➨ Do you feel stuck in a role?
➨ What can you do about this?

Process and task

How things get done in a group is called *process*. What gets done is called *task, content, project, objective* or the *purpose of the group*.

Group process is about taking care of the group and the people in it. Awareness of the process is often missing in groups because we often find it difficult and uncomfortable to give our attention to how we and others are behaving. *Group task* is about getting the job completed and the purpose fulfilled. *Getting on with the job* and *dealing with the nuts and bolts* are the comments used.

Process issues may be dismissed as a waste of time when we should be getting the job done.

Process = feminine, night, yin
Task = masculine, day, yang

A balance needs to be maintained between process and task. If the balance is towards process, more time will be spent on how things are done in the group and how people are feeling about themselves, others and the group. There will be more sharing and contribution from all group members. Participants who are keen to get on with the action may feel impatient with the slower pace. If the balance is towards task, more time will be spent allocating tasks, receiving information and data, setting deadlines and sorting out practical details. The pace may be faster and people will be concentrating on analysis and actions rather than feelings. Some group members may not be participating and may feel left out. There is no correct balance. However, most project groups do not pay enough attention to process.

Thinking Points

- ➠ How do you see the balance of process and task in your group?
- ➠ Would you like the balance to be more towards process or task?
- ➠ How do other members see the balance?
- ➠ Would they like more accent on task or process?
- ➠ Is everyone in the group participating?
- ➠ Does it matter to you?

The role of the facilitator is to guide the process of the group so it is as easy as possible for the group to achieve its task. A facilitator seeks to balance process and task. See also Chapter 6, Guidelines for a Facilitator.

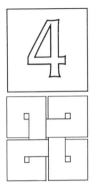

Group Development

This chapter covers areas of development which will allow groups to move through the *Schooldays* and *Teenage Adjustment Stages* and enter the *Maturity Stage, Getting to Synergy*. By attending to these issues in advance, you can avoid much conflict. These are the issues on which many groups get stuck and founder.

Group purpose

Each group has a purpose. You need to discuss and clarify this so that all the group members are aligned with it. Processes such as a structured round, Tool 2, or a brainstorm, Tool 3, can be useful. If the purpose remains unclear, you may discover there is no purpose in having the group.

Usually the purpose of the group can be expressed in one sentence. Keep it short and focused. For example:

> *To produce a five-year strategic plan.*
> *To develop and maintain a loving and*
> *nurturing family.*

To set up a holiday program in our neighborhood.
To build a community center in our community.

Make sure the purpose is written down and available to all group members.

As well as a group purpose, it is useful to develop specific group projects which lead towards realizing the group purpose. Projects need to have clear results and time frames. They need to be written down and tasks assigned to specific group members who report back to the whole group regularly on progress.

Formal project teams will do this through setting specific objectives and tasks within the context of time lines which meet the overall project requirements.

Group projects keep a group focused and grounded. Members know what they are up to, what they are achieving, and what is working or not working. Carrying out and completing projects gives the group a sense of progress, development and achievement.

A project for a family group could be:

To have a summer vacation at the beach by _____ (date).

Tasks for planning and organizing the vacation are then allocated, written down and reviewed each week at a regular family meeting.

Thinking Points

- ➡ What is the purpose of this group?
- ➡ What are we meeting for?
- ➡ How do we know when our purpose is achieved?
- ➡ Is this group purpose important to me?
- ➡ Do we have projects which will lead to the fulfillment of the group purpose?

Values

Underlying a group purpose are some values about things which have brought the group together. It will be useful to identify these values and seek agreement on the most relevant and important to your group purpose. Keep the list short.

Differences in values, if unexpressed, can lead to later conflict. If you clarify values at an early stage, you can avoid some later misunderstandings and upsets. Here is a list of values which may be a useful starting point for generating your group's list. These are the values which are the foundation of this book:

Cooperative decision-making

Open expression of feelings

Punctuality

Attendance at all group meetings

Diversity of ideas and thoughts

Honesty

Commitment to reach agreement

Expression of acknowledgment

Getting results

Congruence between speaking and action

Accountability

Full participation

Autonomy

Ways of identifying values include techniques such as rounds and brainstorming. See Tools 1, 2 and 3. For another exercise, see Tool 8.

➠ What do we value that has us establish this group purpose?
➠ What are our beliefs and ideas about it?
➠ Am I clear why I value this group?
➠ Have I been honest about my values?
➠ Am I withholding anything that is important to me and may come up as an issue later?

Commitment and setting limits

A way of managing your participation in a group is for you to clearly understand how much time it will take, why you are there (the purpose of the group), and the importance (value) of the group purpose in relation to your personal values and priorities.

As well as the time needed for group meetings, it will be useful for you to understand other commitments such as time to be allocated outside meetings, and resources needed such as financial support, transportation, skills and equipment. You may want to set some limits on your involvement:

> *I can allocate_____hours a week/month.*
> *The resources I will supply are_____.*
> *I will not contribute or supply_____.*

Find out as much as possible at the beginning and be comfortable about saying *no* to further requests which are outside your limits. If you are not sure, ask for time to consider any further commitment:

> *I will think it over and let you know by_____(date).*

It is also helpful to find out when the group will end:

> *Is the project planned to be completed by_____(date)?*
> *Is the support group to be set up for_____weeks and to be reviewed?*

Ground rules

A useful way to clarify the way a group will operate (group process) is to set ground rules at the first or second meeting. Ground rules can include:

- ☐ Being on time and present at all meetings (sessions).
- ☐ Confidentiality of all personal content.
- ☐ No smoking or swearing.
- ☐ Each person is responsible for their own comfort in the group.
- ☐ Each person is responsible for expressing their own needs (physical, emotional or relating to group task or process).
- ☐ Speaking for ourselves (*I feel, I think*) not others (*We feel, we think*).

Ground rules are best kept to a minimum. They need to be written down and displayed.

If ground rules are broken, any group member can draw attention to the lapse and request recommitment. Drawing attention to broken ground rules early in the life of the group helps to educate and remind group members.

Ground rules need to *matter* or it is best not to set them.

Joining and leaving

If a group has a closed membership, it is important that adding any new member is agreed to and negotiated with the whole group. It is important that agreement is not assumed, but specifically discussed and agreement reached. Failure to do this can lead to underlying resentment which may never be expressed.

New group members need to be welcomed and feel comfortable before they can participate fully. One way of bringing a new member *up to speed* quickly is to assign him or her a *buddy* to bring them up to date outside the group.

It is important for someone leaving a group to *take leave of it,* as with a one-to-one relationship. Saying good-bye and acknowledging the contribution of the group helps both the leader and the group to move on.

Thinking Points

➠ Do I have agreement to join (or take a guest to) the group?
➠ Am I complete with the group? (Have I nothing left to say on leaving or have I collected added baggage?)

Encouraging participation

Full participation is a function of a healthy group. When you meet with any group it indicates that you are involved and ready to participate. However, often you are not ready to be fully committed. One of the powerful things a facilitator or group member can do is to ensure that everyone participates and speaks early in a group session. Speaking in itself creates participation. Hearing ourselves speak gives us confidence that we belong and are accepted.

Warmup exercises are useful for new groups and at the beginning of group sessions. See Tools 14-20 and Tools 21-25.

Some groups will have beginning rituals such as a welcome by a senior person or a group practice which will serve the warm-up purpose as well as establish (or claim) space for the group. See Rituals, page 34.

Rounds and brainstorming are useful techniques to encourage participation. If only a few people are taking part, it can be useful to have a session of paired sharing to get members talking again. See Tool 4. A direct question to non-sharers is also helpful:

What do you think, Doris?
What is your opinion, Bill?

A general request for contribution can also be made *from anyone who hasn't spoken so far.* It is best not to force contribution. Some people naturally talk more than others.

Often it will be easy for you to tell if someone would like to share by observing their body language:

☐ Leaning forward
☐ Clearing their throat
☐ Biting their lip
☐ Facial expressions

Sometimes people are reluctant to speak because they don't know or have forgotten others' names. It helps to wear name tags or do name exercises often to remind people. See Tools 14-20.

Open agenda-setting, Chapter 8, page 70, will also encourage participation. Accepting silence is helpful in allowing space for quiet people to contribute.

Agenda-setting

It is useful for a group to choose how to develop the agenda at the first or second meeting. Some of the alternatives are:

Open agenda—generated at the beginning of the meeting with participation from all group members.
Prearranged agenda—presented to the meeting by the facilitator or chairperson with opportunity for additions.
Prearranged and circulated agenda—with sufficient notice to allow people time to prepare relevant material for the meeting.

Different kinds of groups will choose different alternatives. A family or support group may prefer an open agenda, while a project work group may prefer a prearranged and circulated agenda. Another question to address is who will prepare the prearranged agenda and who will be consulted? If you ensure choices are made in advance, you can avoid later upset.

Decision-making

There are a number of decision-making alternatives. Choose the one or more which will suit your group:

Collective (or consensus) decision-making

Collective decision-making is based on an *agreement to reach agreement* by the whole group on all decisions made. All group members have the right to choose to participate or not in all decisions. Such agreements will vary and may include some of the following:

- ☐ Everyone is actively involved in all decisions.
- ☐ Those directly affected by a decision are involved in the decision. (All group members agree in advance what *directly affected* means.)
- ☐ All disagreements must be worked through before action is taken or disagreements can be noted and not hold up action if all group members agree to this for a specific decision (agree to disagree).
- ☐ Agreement by the whole group that individuals or subgroups can make decisions within agreed limits.

A process for reaching agreement is described in Chapter 8, Discussion and action-planning, page 71. Collective decision-making is preferred by the authors as it draws out the collective wisdom of the group and encourages each group member to take responsibility for all decisions made. Collective decision-making may take time at first but with practice can be quick. This mode of decision-making allows for synergy to occur.

Majority decision-making

A vote is taken and the majority choice becomes the decision. The chairperson may have a vote if the voting is even. This is the decision-making mode of committees and is set out in formal committee rules. This mode is quick and easy but tends to lead to the development of factions and resentments over time. Consistently outvoted factions feel powerless and frustrated.

Individual decision-making

One person decides on behalf of the whole group. This mode is quick and most appropriate for routine tasks. It is also useful in an emergency but tends to undermine the power and effectiveness of the group if used frequently or without agreement. This is the usual practice of hierarchical organizations.

Subgroup decision-making

Decisions are made in subgroups by designated key people (using collective or majority decision-making). This is a useful mode for specific tasks or parts of a larger project.

There are many variations or combinations of these four decision-making modes. For example:

> Robert's business uses majority decision-making as its primary mode but uses collective decision-making for major policy decisions such as expansion of major new markets. Routine and emergency decisions are made by individual decision-making within preagreed limits.

It is important for each new group to choose how decisions will be made at the first or early meetings. Use collective decision-making for this initial decision.

➠ What is the primary decision-making mode in your group?
➠ How does this decision-making mode affect the group?
➠ Which decision-making mode do you feel most comfortable with and why?
➠ How did your group decide on a decision-making mode?
➠ Are there times when different modes would be useful?

Support systems

There are many ways that people can support one another in groups. You may like to design your own, but here are some ideas:

Buddy system

Two group members buddy one another to encourage and remind one another between meetings of tasks and commitments taken on in the group. This is a reciprocal system. Regular phone calls can be useful.

Coaching system

Group members choose a person who will coach them on keeping their commitments and/or desired changes in behavior. This can be a more experienced group member or someone outside the group. Such coaching will be asked for by the group member (not the coach).

Mentoring

This is similar to a coaching system. A mentor may be a longer-term relationship and not dependent on any particular group involvement. A mentor is usually an older, more experienced person you admire and who can advise and assist you in meeting your career or life objectives.

Support groups

A group of people meet to provide support and coaching to one another. This may be a professional support group, discussed in Chapter 8, page 73, or a personal-development support group, page 76.

Rituals

Rituals are a powerful way of building group identity and tapping into the full or synergistic potential of the group. Another term for this could be *higher purpose.*

Rituals are not rational. They will take you outside or past your normal thinking. They will expand your awareness and give you access to an energy of which you are usually only dimly conscious.

Most established groups have ritual elements. Consider the rituals associated with service clubs, lodges, Scouts, churches, schools and universities. Rituals recognize that a group is more than the individual members who are present at the time.

Rituals develop naturally over time. They can also be consciously added to any group. The most effective rituals are usually those developed by the group members themselves. Rituals from other sources can provide ideas or even be adapted. There are some interesting books on rituals which you may like to read (see Bibliography).

Welcoming, singing, chanting, dancing, use of secret hand-shakes and signs can all be part of ritual activities. Rituals need not be heavy or serious. They can be light and fun—such as a basketball team *whoop* before a game. Too much ritual can slow down the group and lead to boredom and stagnation.

Thinking Points

➠ Do I feel comfortable with rituals?
➠ Has the group already developed some rituals?
➠ What are they? Are the group rituals useful?
➠ Do they reflect the group purpose?
➠ What rituals can we create or adapt for our group?
➠ What is the higher purpose of our group?

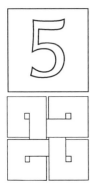

5 People in Groups

Being Present

Each person in a group is different and comes to the group with his or her own set of baggage. When individuals interact in a group they often trip over their own or each other's baggage—(ideas, beliefs, hang-ups, desires, tragedies, hopes, fears, and so on). How does this occur? Here is an example:

> Barbara mentions that on her way to the meeting she saw a man hitting a woman. There is another woman in the group whose father used to hit her mother and her when she was a child. Their family life was unhappy. A man in the group hit a woman during an argument when he was a teenager. He still feels guilty about this. A person in the group is afraid that a friend of hers could be the man referred to by Barbara, as he lives nearby.
>
> All three group members are *tripped up* or *triggered* by Barbara's comment and immediately become mentally absent from the group for some minutes.

Here is another example:

> David mentions in his work group that he has just had a conversation with his manager about a new project. One person in the group dislikes this manager intensely. The manager shouted at him the previous day in front of other staff members. Another person in the group is concerned about the new project taking resources away from his own project.
>
> Both group members are triggered by David's comment and mentally leave the group to dwell on their concerns. One does not contribute to the conversation for 10 minutes. The other responds negatively to three suggestions made by David.

A further example:

> Donna mentions in her group that she wants to put the topic *Planning* on the agenda. One person in the group is planning an overseas trip and spent the previous evening looking through brochures with her husband. On hearing the word *Planning* she remembers the previous evening with pleasure and starts to daydream about the overseas trip. When asked for her opinion as part of the group discussion she is unable to respond because she has not heard the conversation.

Do you get the idea? We get tripped up by things others say. Some people are tripped up most of the time. Most people get tripped up at least once every few minutes. If you are aware, you can *reconnect yourself* quickly, say within 30 seconds. This takes skill and practice.

Getting tripped up takes your attention away from the group and the present. You are not *all there—you are out to lunch.* You may miss part of the conversation or it may go in one ear and out the other. In a group there will nearly always be a number of people who are *not all there* (fully present).

Here are some topics which are very likely to trip people up:

Sex/sexism	Politics	Money
Violence	School	Babies
Death	Racism	Divorce
Relationships	Taxes	Illness

Thinking Points

➠ Do I notice when I get tripped up by things others say?
➠ Do I notice when others get tripped up?
➠ What are the main topics which trip me up?
➠ What ways can I think of that I can use to reconnect myself when I get triggered?

Speaking and listening

For each group member, being in a group is mainly about speaking and listening. This is the bread and butter of being in a group.

The area of communication skills is a large one and not the specific focus of this book. There are lots of ways of training yourself in speaking and listening skills and all group members are encouraged to do this. Training opportunities include courses, seminars, books and videos on assertiveness and communication.

There are also other communication and personal-development courses which will shift or transform your speaking and listening. Some useful points about speaking and listening are:

- ☐ **Use open rather than closed questions:**
  What do you think about this? (an open question) encourages conversation and requires more than a yes or no answer. This contrasts with *Do you agree with this?* (a closed question because it only needs a yes or no answer).

- ☐ **Use I statements, unless speaking for others with their specific agreement:**
  I think rather than *We think.*
  I feel angry that . . . rather than *We all feel angry that . . .*

- ☐ **Use reflective listening:**
  Are you saying that . . . (summary to check for understanding)?
  Do you mean that . . . ?

- ☐ **Watch for listening blocks such as:**
  Comparing yourself to the speaker.
  Comparing the speaker to others.
  Thinking about what you are going to say next.
  Daydreaming.
  Making up advice for someone rather than listening to them.
  Knowing it already.
  Saying: *Something similar happened to me . . .*
  Jumping to conclusions.
  Mindreading.

- ☐ **Watch for speaking blocks such as:**
  It's not that important.
  I'll tell them next week.
  I've said it once and I won't say it again.
  I'd say it but I know they won't listen.
  No one ever listens to me.
  They must know what I think by now.

☐ **A powerful listener is a person about whom people say:**

When I was with Brad I found myself saying things I've never allowed myself to say before.

I felt really heard.

I felt affirmed and acknowledged.

We had a great conversation—even though the listener didn't say much at all.

☐ **A powerful speaker is one about whom people say:**

I heard every word they said.

You could have heard a pin drop.

I've never found that topic interesting before. Now I want to know more.

You must meet Carmen. She is inspiring.

Group exercises on speaking and listening are included in Tools 32-37.

Withholding

We all withhold part of ourselves from others. We are afraid to reveal ourselves fully. If we spoke all of our internal dialogue out loud in a group, there would be such a hubbub that it would be impossible to get anything done. Withholding includes the way we usually keep quiet about sexual attraction and repulsion and violent or highly critical thoughts about others.

Some encounter and therapy groups specialize in encouraging members to let everything come out. But withholding is not always a bad idea, although it can make us weird. For example, when we withhold powerful sexual attraction we tend to act strangely, maybe even giving the person we are attracted to the impression we don't like them.

Like most people in groups, including family groups, you are probably always censoring what you share and what you withhold. This is a pity, because the level of intimacy and energy is directly related to the depth of sharing.

A way to address withholding is to begin to notice what you share or withhold. You can do this by watching, observing and noticing what you say. If you do this over a period of time, withholding can become more of a conscious choice. Once you are able to choose consciously, you can play and experiment with sharing more or less of your thoughts and feelings.

I feel hurt that you didn't do anything with my suggestion.
I am angry that you criticized me when I wasn't here.
I am sad that you are going away for three months. I will miss you.

You and other group members need to share disagreement with the group process and decisions or if you don't understand something. It is also important for everyone to share feelings that are getting in the way of their being active participants. Sharing feeling withholds is a powerful way to increase group intimacy and energy. See Tool 30.

Thinking Points _____

- ➠ What is getting in the way of my contribution to the group?
- ➠ What thoughts and feelings are getting in the way?
- ➠ Can I put these to one side and contribute anyway?
- ➠ Which of my thoughts and feelings am I able to share so that I can be more fully present?
- ➠ How risky is sharing my thoughts and feelings?

Hidden agendas

Most people have some things they want out of a group that they are not prepared to share—these are *hidden agendas.* Hidden agendas are part of your baggage and you need to be aware of your own and be tolerant of those of others. When trust has deepened, your group may like to experiment sharing hidden agendas as a starting exercise or when the energy of the group is becoming low.

Hidden agendas can be such things as:

> *I joined this group because I am a friend of (or am attracted to) Lorraine and Bill and I want to get to know them better.*
> *I am only here because I have to be (family group or work meeting).*
> *I would like the meeting to be short so I can get back to doing . . . which I enjoy.*
> *I want you all to like and admire me and become my friend.*
> *I want to make a major contribution to this group so I will look good to my manager and improve my promotion chances.*

Attraction and repulsion

You will be attracted to some people and you will be repelled by others. This occurs in all groups.

> ***Most attraction and repulsion between people
> has to do with the past.***

Looking through your baggage, you assess, judge, and have opinions about yourself and everyone else based on what has happened in the past. Attraction and repulsion can range all the way from mild to intense. Attraction and repulsion are to do with *you*, not the other person.

Think about a member of a group you belong to. Take time now to try this identity check:

Who does he remind me of?
How is she like them?
How is he different?

Identity check

An in-depth identity check is useful if you are beginning a close working or personal relationship or if a relationship is becoming difficult or stuck. It goes as follows:

Sit opposite one another on the same level and maintain eye contact. Person A asks B the following questions and encourages B to answer them as fully as possible:

Who do I remind you of?
How am I like . . . (say name of person)?
What do you want to say to (name)? Say it to me now as if I were him.
What do you want (name) to say to you? (Person A then responds to B as though B was that person.)
How am I different from that person? (Continue asking this question until both of you are clear that you are quite distinct from that person.)

You may find that a person reminds you of more than one other and the whole process will need to be repeated. When Person B has completed the process, swap roles and begin again.

Conflict

Conflict in groups is inevitable. Given our tendency to get tripped up by our own baggage and our attraction/repulsion towards other people, it is to be expected that disagreements will occur in groups. Conflict is normal and is best handled by taking care of it at once. Conflict can range from mild disagreement to angry outbursts. Violence, however, is never acceptable in groups.

If you do not take care of conflict it can lead to resentment, lack of cooperation, lack of energy, people avoiding one another, indirect attacks, and subversion in groups. A highly creative group or an issues-related group is likely to have a higher degree of conflict than some others. Lack of any conflict in a group may indicate apathy, lack of interest, boredom, people feeling unsafe to share, and low self-esteem of group members.

Working through and resolving conflict calls for sensitive and creative facilitation. The art is in knowing when to intervene and when to suggest a process to assist the group. There is no right answer. Each facilitator will intervene differently.

Remember, the group can work it out and each person in the group has an important role to play. If you as facilitator or group member take this approach, then it will reduce the likelihood of group members feeling hurt or damaged by the conflict.

Most of us are scared of open conflict and avoid it if we can. There is a risk to expressing and working through conflict. If the working through involves harsh words and name-calling, people can feel deeply hurt and relationships can be damaged, sometimes permanently. Some group members may be afraid that if they really express their anger, they may go out of control and become violent, or that others may do this. These fears can be very real and are based on experience.

So why take the risk? Why not avoid conflict at all costs? Conflict is rather like disease. Prevention is best. That means attending to areas where disagreement may occur before they become an issue. If you have not prevented a conflict from happening, your next choice is to treat it early—or hope it goes away. If it goes away over time, fine. If it doesn't, then you will still have to handle it, and it is likely to be more serious.

Another analogy for handling conflict is the way you look after your car. If you take care of it, doing things like putting in oil and water, and getting the car serviced, you avoid a lot of problems. If something goes wrong, you can ignore it and hope it goes away or take remedial action. If you do nothing and wait, you might end up with a blown-up engine or have a nasty accident.

So handling conflict is very like your physical health or car maintenance. Prevention is much better than cure.

Preventive action

Think about, talk about and take action on the sections in this book which apply to your group, particularly group purpose, values, joining and leaving, ground rules, and decision-making, as outlined in Chapter 4, Group Development. Keep an eye to the future. What might go wrong if you don't take action now? Preventive action is about planning and applying the group plan.

Early action

Group members have begun to snap at one another, go quiet suddenly, miss meetings, sulk or look tense or bored. Or perhaps some are avoiding eye contact or are not talking to one another. Someone may have left the room suddenly, banging the door. Something is *wrong* and you can feel it. This is when a choice needs to be made. Do you handle it now or wait? It is a choice, but given people's normal tendency to avoid conflict, we recommend you act now and don't put it off.

Early action can be very simple. Just say how you are feeling and encourage others to do the same. You could say:

> *I'm feeling uncomfortable/upset about . . . I'd like us to talk about it now.*

Or to someone who appears upset or uneasy:

> *Dale, are you uncomfortable about something?*

Or make a general comment like:

> *What's going on in the group right now?*

This will open up the subject and get people sharing about it. Encourage participants to separate what happened from their feelings about it:

> *Bill agreed to do (task) by (time) and he didn't do it. I feel . . .* rather than: *I'm annoyed with Bill. He can't be trusted. He couldn't even be relied on to do . . . (task) on time.*

If a number of people are upset about the same thing, give several of them an opportunity to speak and then ask Bill to respond:

> *Tell us what happened, Bill.*

Encourage Bill to respond with the facts:

> *I didn't get it done by the time I promised. I phoned Anne and told her that I'd have it done by . . . I'm sorry to let you all down.*

Discourage Bill from a reaction that doesn't address the issue, such as:

> *You people obviously don't trust me.*

This kind of interchange won't take long if kept to facts and clear expression of feelings. Make sure the interchange ends with a promise or new decision if this is needed. If your intervention has opened up a can of worms—a more serious conflict—read on.

Full conflict

There are probably several things going on at once and several issues may have come up. Someone may be angry and another defensive, while others are confused and apprehensive. What do you do?

You now need a *facilitator*. If the group does not have one, you may like to bring one in. Or if the conflict cannot wait, it may need to be you—the one with this book. The first thing to remember is: Don't panic! Together the group can work it through—and in working it through, gain in maturity. Say to the rest of the group:

Hey, we have a conflict here. Let's work through it.

What you are doing by saying this is naming what is happening and suggesting an intervention. This helps to give the group as a whole some clarity and power.

Now is the time to suggest a technique or process. It will help if you have already read the Toolkit. Or you may need to call a coffee break at this stage. Actually, using a break as a technique can be useful at these times because it gives people a chance to cool off.

The two most helpful parts of the Toolkit at this stage are A, Tools for Generating Ideas and Exploring Issues, and P, Tools for Resolving Conflict. Choose a technique with agreement from the group and use it. By stopping and choosing a process or technique, the group will become a little more rational. Choosing involves putting down our individual baggage and focusing our attention on the *greater good* of the whole group.

If you are an inexperienced facilitator, you may be afraid that a technique won't work or that you might end up looking foolish. This is natural and it will help if you share this concern with the group. If it does happen that the conflict is not completely worked through, summarize where the group has gotten to and check for agreement. Identify with the group what the next step could be.

- ☐ Key players could meet and come back with a proposed course of action to the next meeting.
- ☐ The issue could be addressed again at the next meeting.
- ☐ Call a special meeting to address the issue.
- ☐ Discuss what resource, people or information are missing which will help to resolve the issue.
- ☐ Have a group scream.

Thinking Points

- ⇨ Am I able to share with others when I am uncomfortable or upset? If not, what gets in the way?
- ⇨ Can I identify examples of avoidance, indirect attacks and subversion in the group?
- ⇨ Is conflict okay?

Physical contact

People have different behaviors and expectations about touching other people in groups. Some groups have a high level of physical contact while others have none. Some people require a lot of physical space between them and other group members and feel crowded or threatened by close contact. Other people do not mind someone sitting or standing close to them. Work groups often have less touching than social or family groups. Women are more inclined to hug one another than men. Some ethnic cultures have a lot more touching than others.

If touching or lack of it in your group feels uncomfortable, it is helpful to talk about it in the group.

Thinking Points

➡ How much physical contact do you expect to receive or give in your group?
➡ How much personal space do you expect or give to others?
➡ How do you feel if someone touches you or sits close to you?
➡ What is your interpretation of this?

Being an effective group member

Here are some useful hints for being an effective group member. Remember there is no right way to be in a group. On the contrary, diversity is what makes a group interesting.

☐ Get to know the other people. A friendly interest in other members helps to build a climate of trust and openness in the group. Use names and don't be afraid to ask if you forget.

☐ Be clear about the group purpose, values, ground rules and practices. Also be clear about your commitments in time and energy and the limits to your involvement.

☐ Contribute to discussions, group decision-making and task allocation. Your contribution is needed for the group to be all it can be.

- [ ] Share yourself, your thoughts, ideas, feelings, and concerns. Your personality adds to the richness of the group.

- [ ] Listen generously to other people. Remember that each person is committed to the group purpose, even if his or her baggage is getting in the way.

- [ ] Speak concisely and to the point. Make sure you can be heard and remember time is precious. Don't ramble on.

- [ ] Start to recognize when you get tripped up by your own or others' baggage. If you can, bring yourself back quickly to the present. If you can't, share your trip-up with the other group members.

- [ ] Be proactive. Take an initiating role when you can. Make suggestions, propose alternatives, look for what's missing in the discussion and add it. Being proactive takes being awake and present.

- [ ] Be flexible. Avoid taking a fixed position. Remember there is no one right way. Be prepared to negotiate no matter how strongly you feel about something.

- [ ] If you don't understand or have missed something, admit it. You need to understand the conversation if you are going to contribute to it.

- [ ] Don't avoid conflict. Disagreement and conflict are an important part of the development of the group. See conflict as a way through to a more useful solution.

- [ ] Keep to the ground rules and encourage others to keep to them too. If the ground rules are not working, initiate a discussion to remind the group, or if needed, revise the ground rules.

☐ Fulfill your commitments. Do what you say you will do by the time you promised.

☐ Go to all group meetings clear and ready for action.

☐ Leave group meetings clear with nothing left unsaid. Check at the end of the meeting that you have not accumulated any more baggage.

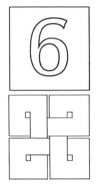

Guidelines for a Facilitator

Group facilitation is the art of guiding the group process towards the agreed objectives. A facilitator guides the process and does not get involved in content. A facilitator intervenes to protect the group process and keep the group on track to fulfill its task.

There is no recipe for a facilitator to follow and there is no one right way to facilitate a group. But there are guidelines, techniques and tips which you may find useful. There are *safety precautions* you can take. It is a bit like being a mountain guide when each new group is traversing a different mountain.

You may have a general idea of how it might go based on previous experience. You know how to avoid danger and pitfalls. You have checked the weather and your equipment. You have had first-aid training. However, you cannot be sure what the way will be like or when danger will arise. Facilitating groups is like this.

Groups are made up of individual people. People are unpredictable—groups of people can be very unpredictable. The rest of this chapter sets out some guidelines for being an effective facilitator.

Be awake
Your most important asset as a facilitator is your awareness. Being *awake* and *present* to each moment, moment by moment—listening, looking, sensing—100 percent present. Personal development work, meditation, consciousness-raising, discussion, training and development in experiential learning techniques are all useful ways to develop awareness. Experiment to find ways that work for you.

Be adaptable
There is no one sure-fire technique that will always work at a particular time for the group—not even if you know every technique there is to know. It is a matter of choosing what to do in a particular moment: whether to intervene or not, and how to intervene at that time. You can plan ahead but you always need to be ready to adapt to what is happening at the moment.

If you don't know, say so
If you don't know what to suggest or do when an intervention seems to be needed in a group, say so and ask for suggestions. Someone else may have a good idea or their suggestion may spark an idea for you. Don't pretend you know everything—nobody does.

Trust the resources of the group
The facilitator trusts that the group will have the resources to

achieve its task and work through any process issues. Trust in this sense is an attitude of confidence that the resources are present and will be discovered. The facilitator enables the group to explore and find the resources. This is the way a group becomes empowered. This does not mean that the task will always be fulfilled. It means not giving up when the going gets tough and perhaps all group members are wilting.

Honor each group member

Facilitation is about honoring each group member and encouraging full participation while having the group task achieved effectively and efficiently. Always approach group members as capable, aware and fully functioning people who are committed to the group purpose. Even if they are behaving in disruptive ways, always treat them as if they were acting honorably and for the good of the group.

Tap group energy

A group is capable of more than any one member thinks. Remember: One + one + one + one = five or more. This is the equation of synergy. We really have no idea what we can achieve in a group. Maybe we can achieve almost anything in the world as a group. It may take some ingenuity to discover how we can achieve it. An effective facilitator knows that group members are stopped mainly by baggage from the past and can achieve amazing results. The facilitator is out to tap the energy of the group and tap into the group synergy.

Be yourself

As a facilitator, you will be most effective when you are being your natural self and allowing your own personality to be expressed. People get permission to be themselves from the way a facilitator behaves—that is, through modeling. If you are stiff and formal, the group tends to be like that. If you are relaxed and self-expressed, the group tends to be like that too.

Thinking Points _____

- ⇒ How is the group being?
- ⇒ How does this reflect you?
- ⇒ Are you expressing yourself and remaining focused on the group task?

(Keep checking to see how the group is reflecting how you are being.)

Develop discernment
Make sure your eyes and ears are open all the time. Listen and see without judgment, but with discernment.

Thinking Points _____

- ⇒ When is a person tripped up?
- ⇒ When is a person asleep, upset, caught in a pattern or triggered?
- ⇒ When are two or more people tripping up one another?
- ⇒ Are they aware of it?
- ⇒ Do they want to stop?
- ⇒ Who has given up and why?
- ⇒ Who is raring to go and frustrated by the non-action of others?

(Discern when these behaviors are present and if an intervention is necessary.)

Keep intervention to a minimum

Intervene only when it is necessary to behavior which is:

- ☐ Impeding progress without the agreement of the group.
- ☐ Off track in the discussion and the result of someone having tripped over baggage from the past.
- ☐ Undermining the possibility of group synergy (see Chapter 7).
- ☐ Physically dangerous.

Monitor the energy level

Monitor the energy level of the group at all times. This is your barometer. Energy is indicated by tone of voice, body posture, eye contact, level or participation and level of activity directed towards the task. Are people awake or asleep, engaged or disengaged? The energy of a group will alter all the time.

At the beginning of a day people often have lots of energy. After lunch they are often low in energy. Short breaks or active exercises can help keep energy up for longer sessions. For most people, concentration is hard to maintain for longer than 30 to 40 minutes. Use some active exercise when energy is low and the meeting is long. See Tools 63-67.

Stay clear

This is similar to being awake and present moment by moment. As a facilitator, notice when you get tripped up by your own or others' baggage. When you do get tripped up, note the *trigger* word(s) for you to work through later. Reconnect yourself quickly and carry on. Don't take personally, or get drawn into any comment, ideas or beliefs expressed in the group, nor any criticism, no matter how personal. If you get triggered and can't reconnect quickly, tell the group you are triggered and call a short break. Then:

- [ ] Take an uninvolved group member aside and ask them to ask you: *What do you need to say or do to get clear?* You will probably be feeling angry and need to express this in some way. You may prefer to do this in another room, by jumping up and down or screaming into a towel.
- [ ] If it is inappropriate to use a group member, ask yourself the question and take similar action.

Get the job done

Always remember you are there to get the job done. Make sure you know the purpose of the group and the desired outcomes for the meeting. Check how much time the group is prepared to spend on group process issues. Do you know the values of the group? Are they clearly stated? Do the values indicate a balance between process and task?

Don't be attached to your own interventions

You may come up with a brilliant intervention but, if it doesn't work, drop it. Only use an intervention to keep the group focused, not because you think it is a brilliant insight. Your job is not to show how smart you are.

Take everything that occurs as relevant

A facilitator takes everything that is said or done in the group as group interaction, including individual exchanges, side comments, and accidental occurrences. For example, if someone falls off his chair, that becomes part of the group process rather than an interruption. Some facilitators use outside interruptions as well, like someone coming into the room accidentally.

Improvise

Facilitation is an improvisational art within an agreed and negotiated structure. It is like jazz rather than classical music. Don't get stuck in doing things a certain way. Remember there is no one way or technique. Be flexible and stay awake.

When in doubt, check it out

When in doubt, check it out is a useful guideline for a facilitator. If you are not sure that everyone is in agreement with a decision or task, ask if everyone agrees. If necessary, request a response from everyone—a *yes* or a *no*. Silence does not necessarily mean assent.

Seek agreement

A facilitator seeks agreement from everyone and uses collective decision-making processes (consensus) unless there is agreement by everyone to do otherwise. Voting, majority or otherwise, is not a recommended way of reaching a decision in a facilitated group.

Use questions and suggestions

Questions and suggestions are the usual way a facilitator intervenes. Avoid giving advice. Say *I suggest* rather than *What you should do is* . . . . Also avoid giving the answer to an issue. Your job as facilitator is to guide the process, not be involved in the content, even if you are positive you know the answer.

Negotiate and contract

A facilitator is an effective negotiator within groups. The structure and framework of meetings, processes and so on are developed through negotiation. Proposals and counter proposals are encouraged until agreement is reached. Agreement equals the contract. Most group decisions—including ground rules, time limits, personal responsibilities, roles, commitment, membership, values, purpose, aims, objectives and evaluation methods—are negotiated.

Be culturally sensitive

Cultural sensitivity is essential. Knowledge of the customs, rituals, and sensitivities of people from cultures other than your own is most important. If you do not have this knowledge you need to say so. Seek advice from people in the group to ensure that cultural sensitivity is honored. Community sensitivities also need to be addressed in a similar way. Don't assume—ask.

Start well

Group meetings and workshops have a beginning, a middle and an end. Getting started is like setting out on a journey or laying the foundation of a house. The first part of a group meeting or workshop is critical to the whole process and time needs to be allowed for the process of starting. See Chapter 8 and Tools 21-25.

Work with conflict

A facilitator is comfortable with conflict and always encourages it to be expressed openly. Disagreement is the natural result of different personalities, different views and opinions. If a group is to develop to maturity, it will need to work with conflict, rather than avoid it.

Creative conflict resolution can be synergistic and lead to major breakthroughs and forward movement in a group. Remember— don't get tripped up by conflict or get involved in the content.

Invite feedback

A facilitator invites feedback during and at the end of group meetings. All feedback is useful. Specific comments are more useful than general ones. One feedback technique is the use of rounds of negative and positive comments. See Tools 12 and 13.

Acknowledge and affirm

A facilitator gives frequent acknowledgment and affirmation. Encourage your group to keep going during long or difficult processes by affirming progress and acknowledging completion of tasks. Model the giving of acknowledgment and affirmation and encourage group members to affirm and acknowledge one another. See Tools 49-52.

Have a sense of humor

A sense of humor is a great asset to a facilitator. The use of humor can usefully defuse some tense moments. There is nothing better than a light touch at the appropriate time.

Facilitation is Zen

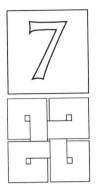

Synergy

What is synergy?

In Chapter 1 we wrote about *something special* which can happen in a group of people working together on a project which they all care strongly about and really want to succeed. They are so eager to meet the project objective that no circumstances seem able to stop them. There is a unity and concerted action in the group which enables them to do what they and others thought impossible.

The project could be a couple without any building skills building their own dream house or a sports team with no chance beating the top team. It could be a work team of junior sales-people which produces outstanding results or a community group which takes on the local government and brings about the reversal of a major local-government decision.

Synergy is about tapping into group energy so that the group members are able to accomplish more than they thought possible. People describing their experience of synergy use phrases like:

Things clicked into place.
Things all came together.
We all got energized.
I experienced intimacy and trust.
I forgot my own concerns.
We accepted one another in a new way.
We all joined in spontaneously.
I found myself part of something bigger than me.

Synergistic action is described by musicians and dancers in words such as:

The music played itself.
I was the dance.

Sports team members describe it as:

We just took off.
We were on a roll.
We couldn't do anything wrong.

Tapping into group energy

Tapping into group energy dramatically increases the speed at which a group takes action. It is not about struggling or trying harder. Synergy is rather about flowing and working together harmoniously. Synergy is about speed and flexibility. It is about coordinated action and being inspired by one another.

How can you tap into this group energy in a conscious way rather than by accident? How can you generate the degree of group spirit which seems to be available in synergistic groups? In everyday life we usually feel separate from one another to a greater or lesser degree. We are individuals and different from everyone else. We like it this way. This is a function of the different *baggage* which we each carry with us. It keeps us separate and apart from one another.

The ability to let go of our *baggage* even momentarily allows us to identify with and feel for one another in a more direct way. In a group this can be experienced as trust, closeness, peacefulness, understanding, happiness, joy and exhilaration. These are all aspects of love in its broadest sense. Team activities such as sports and games tap into this experience of group energy. This is what we crave when we are together with other people—this experience of unity, acceptance and trust (love).

Increasing group and facilitation skills will open up the pathway to experiencing synergy in your group. Group skills increase the level of cooperation in a group so people begin to feel for one another and start appreciating and noticing one another's viewpoints rather than assessing, judging and making one another wrong. Group members begin to listen to one another in a new way and start to recognize when they are in tune with the rest of the group. Differences are quickly voiced and worked through. Group members take responsibility for their own baggage and strive to stay *clear* with one another.

It is essential to remember, however, that all the skills you learn from this and other books and teachers will not provide automatic access to synergy. Synergy is not the result of following rules, formulas, or even sticking closely to guidelines. It is more subtle than that. Synergy is something to value and generate. It cannot be forced or struggled for. Force will produce the opposite to synergy—separateness and the rigid taking and defending of positions.

Synergy is Zen. Facilitators train themselves to listen for the subtleties of group energy—what enhances it and what detracts from it. This is the *art of facilitation*. Developing and using the techniques in a skillful way is the *craft*.

Access to synergy can dramatically increase the speed and

effectiveness of groups. Ability to access synergy can make a large difference in organizational effectiveness and in the economy. In a national and global environment of rapid change and complex decision making, effectiveness at all levels becomes a critical factor. Synergy is a human capacity we cannot afford to ignore.

Using group energy

Group energy *is*. It is not good or bad. However, it is a powerful force and can be tapped for good or ill depending upon your purpose and set of values. Large gatherings such as concerts, drama productions, team sports with a large mass of spectators, telethons, political mass meetings and global meditations have access to a large amount of group energy.

There are important issues to consider in relation to the use and misuse of mass energy. These issues include purpose, value systems, power and leadership. What are you tapping into synergy for? The issues of purpose, values, power and leadership need to be addressed in all our groups.

Thinking Points _____

- ⟹ Are group members comfortable and aligned with the group purpose and values?
- ⟹ Are there unresolved power issues which have not yet come out into the open?
- ⟹ What is each person holding back?
- ⟹ What is each person afraid of?

  (These are useful questions for a group to explore and will help bring unexpressed fears and concerns out into the open. Open discussion will also help generate an environment in which synergy can occur.)

Signposts to Group Synergy

Purpose
The group has a clear purpose and group members are committed to it.

Vision
A powerful vision is developed by the group. Building the vision, and recording it in some way, in words, art or music serves as an ongoing inspiration to group members particularly when the going gets tough.

Clarity
The group clarifies roles and commitments such as membership, ground rules, expectations and limits.

Projects
The group invents projects to achieve its purpose with clear accountabilities and action plans.

Identity
Group members develop a strong group identity. Trust is developed through group members sharing themselves honestly with one another. Members honor one another and make allowances for each other's baggage.

Communication
The group finds agreed ways to work through conflict rather than avoiding it. Conflict is seen as normal—feelings are seen as normal. People agree to communicate even when it's hard.

Learning
Group members increase effectiveness by identifying what they have learned as they go along through group process and project monitoring and evaluation.

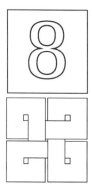

Meeting Models

For Project or Work Groups

Here is a meeting model for project or work groups. You may like to adopt the whole model or just those parts which meet your needs. This model works best for groups of up to 20 people.

Preparation checklist

- ☐ Is a meeting necessary? What are the alternatives?
- ☐ What is the purpose of the meeting? Is it clear?
- ☐ Who needs to be at the meeting? (Key players.)
- ☐ Are the key players available?
- ☐ Decide date, time, and location.
- ☐ Do these arrangements complement the purpose of the meeting?
- ☐ Is a written invitation needed? Telephone?
- ☐ Does an agenda need to be circulated? Discussed? With which key players?
- ☐ Do refreshments need to be arranged for?
- ☐ Meeting facilities?

- □ Transportation?
- □ Interpreters?
- □ Is equipment needed? Chalkboard. Video. Overhead projector. Paper. Pens. (Generate your own list.)
- □ Does resource material need to be circulated? Available before the meeting?
- □ Do any key players need to be reminded?
- □ What outcomes are needed from the meeting?

Environment

Before the meeting, ensure all required resources are prepared and at hand ready to use when appropriate. Prepare the room so that it is clean and welcoming, with tables and chairs set up as you want them for the meeting. Provide only the number of chairs needed.

Arrival

Ensure that people are greeted on arrival and that coats, bags, and so on are attended to. People need time to arrive, greet one another and *get there* both physically and mentally.

The culture of the group (and the organization of which it is a part) is most readily established in the first few minutes of the meeting—even before the meeting proper begins.

Thinking Points

- ⇒ What is the atmosphere you are creating?
- ⇒ Who is responsible for greeting people?
- ⇒ Are people's needs being taken care of?
- ⇒ Do people already know one another or are introductions needed?

Sit in a circle or around a table without any gaps or empty chairs. Ensure everyone is on the same level—not some people on chairs and some on the floor. Make sure everyone is comfortable—not too hot or cold, and air is circulating in the room, and that there are sufficient light and sound levels.

Ensure everyone is close enough to hear the others clearly and see everyone else's face. If someone is seated behind another person, ask him or her to come forward. Rearrange chairs as required. Repeat the request if necessary.

Ritual
There may be a ritual way of starting your meetings that is part of the culture, organization or group.

Establishing roles
Establish who is taking the following roles:

Facilitator: responsible for the group process.

Recorder: records decisions, agenda items, and people present.

Timekeeper: monitors time-frames and ending time of meeting.

Introductions
The facilitator checks with the group to see whether introductions are needed. Introductions are needed if this is a first meeting or if new people have joined the group. If appropriate, the facilitator introduces himself and then invites group members to introduce themselves. This can take the form of a round.

The facilitator checks if everyone is now ready to participate. People may have personal issues—births, deaths, accomplishments, and other items—which they want to share. If a group member is upset or not feeling well, check to see if they would prefer not to attend the meeting. Give him or her the opportunity to leave.

Confirm meeting details

The facilitator confirms:

- [ ] Purpose of the meeting and any required outcomes (be specific).
- [ ] Ending time of meeting.
- [ ] Housekeeping details (food arrangements, breaks, location of toilets).
- [ ] Ground rules. Optional but useful, they need to be clearly understood and agreed by everyone. Examples of ground rules are:

    No smoking in the room.

    Speaking personally and not on behalf of other people— that is, using *I* statements.

    Not interrupting someone when they are speaking.

    Speaking concisely and to the point.

    Not leaving the meeting until it has been completed.

    Starting and finishing on time.

Information sharing

Share short items of information which are relevant to the meeting and which do not require discussion. If discussion occurs, place the item on the agenda. See Open agenda-setting below.

Note: This process is optional and not always useful. If you find people always get into instant discussion, it may be preferable to put each information item on the agenda.

Review previous decisions

Review all decisions made at the previous meeting and check out action taken as a result of decisions. Record the action taken next to each decision. If action has not been taken, bring forward decisions and reenter them in the records of this meeting. If action is no longer practical or relevant, note this next to the decision in previous records. See Records, page 72.

Open agenda-setting

This model is often used by groups using consensus decision-making.

Agenda Items: Each person puts forward the agenda items they want discussed and these are recorded, preferably on a large sheet of paper so everyone can see. The name of the person initiating the agenda item is placed alongside it.

Time-setting: The initiator is asked by the facilitator to estimate how long it will take to discuss the item and the requested time is noted alongside the item. The facilitator checks this time with the meeting, and adjusts if a longer time is required.
    Note: If an initiator nominates five minutes or less for other than an information item it is useful to question this as most items with any discussion at all will take longer. If longer than 30 minutes is requested this also can be questioned.

Priority-setting: The times of all items are added together and the ending time of the meeting checked. If the time needed is longer than the time of the meeting, have a round where each person nominates their two most important agenda items. These can be recorded alongside the item by marking one tick for each person's preferences. This will generate a priority list and items can be addressed in this order. Keep in mind the following:

☐ What items must be discussed today.

☐ What items are important but not urgent.

☐ What items can be left until another meeting or be resolved by another process—such as delegation to one or two people for decision and action.

Discussion and action-planning

Each item is now discussed in turn. The following process may be useful.

☐ The facilitator invites the initiator to:

Introduce the item (issue and background).

Say what they want from the group (feedback, ideas, alternatives or a decision).

Suggest the process or technique they would like the group to use—rounds, brainstorm, pros and cons or continuums. (Tools 1-6.)

☐ The facilitator seeks clarification and group agreement for the request to be implemented. If the initiator is unclear about techniques or processes, the facilitator will suggest one. If specific feedback or ideas are requested, the facilitator may find the technique of rounds useful. Often a round will clarify the issue and common ground and differences will become obvious. An issue can also be explored using pros and cons or brainstorming. Record ideas on large sheets of paper.

☐ When this process is complete, the facilitator summarizes and checks to see what else is needed for the initiator's request to be fulfilled.

☐ If group agreement is needed, request proposals from the

group. Continue this process until a proposal is suggested which meets general agreement. It may be helpful to reach minor agreements along the way. Record these. If a decision is being held up by one or two people, the facilitator can ask what they propose to solve the difficulty. If agreement is still not reached, check with dissenters to see if they are directly affected by the outcome. If not, see if they will allow the decision to be made anyway. Those directly affected by a decision need to be directly involved in the decision making.

☐ The timekeeper keeps an eye on the time and lets the meeting know how it is going: *We have five minutes left on this item.* And *Our time is up.* It is better not to extend time. If time is left at the end of the meeting, you may choose to come back to an item. Act on the assumption that if agreement is going to be reached, it will be reached in the time allowed. Thirty minutes or three hours may not make any difference.

Records
Records of the meeting need to include:

Date/time/location
People present
People absent
Agenda items
Decisions made

Write down each decision as it is reached. Include specific actions, if any, to be taken. Note who will take action on the decision and by when. Always be very specific.

Further meetings
Decide the date, time, location and purpose of any further meetings. Choose facilitator, recorder and timekeeper for the next meeting.

Note: For ongoing groups, an effective system is to rotate roles. Write down a list of names and go through this in order. This saves having to make a decision each time.

Feedback

A closing round may be held in which people express anything that is still incomplete for them from the meeting, or any feedback they would like to give to other members of the group. Check to see if there is anything people need to say or intend to say outside the meeting rather than in it. Encourage them to say it now.

Ending

The group may have a ritual for ending the meeting such as closing remarks by a senior member of the group. The group may wish to design other endings also.

Follow-up

After the meeting, circulate decisions to participants. Alternatively, you may keep a decision book in a central place.

A useful tool between meetings is to set up a decision-management system. This could take the form of *buddies* who coach one another towards taking the action they said they would by the time promised. Another method is to nominate a *decision manager* who keeps in contact with people carrying out decisions and *coaches* them to meet their commitments.

For Professional Support Groups

A professional support group is often small. Three to six members is a workable number. It may include people from the same professional background or people from very different professions who will be able to bring different perspectives and provide useful content from their own area of expertise.

Dale's support group meets for one evening a month and consists of an equal-employment-opportunity consultant, a business advisor, a psychologist, and a facilitator. The facilitator (Dale) is not facilitating the group, but is there as a group member. The group has been meeting for over two years.

Another support group consists of two couples—an arts-center director and her husband who is a doctor, and a real-estate agent and her husband, a computer marketing manager. This group was set up after a communications-training workshop to coach one another in putting the workshop learning into practice. It meets for a breakfast meeting each week, alternating in each other's homes. They have been meeting for more than a year.

Arrival and environment

People arrive (on time), greet one another and seat themselves comfortably in a circle around a low table. Food is available. It may be eaten before, during or after the meeting as agreed by the group.

Allocation of time

Time is allocated to each group member by agreement. It may or may not be equal time at each meeting, but will even out over a period. An order will be established for each person to take a turn.

The completion time is checked or renegotiated as necessary. One person agrees to be the time monitor for the meeting. This role may be rotated.

Individual turns

The person who has the first turn (initiator) states the issue he or she wishes to discuss and outlines it in sufficient detail for the other members to understand it. Other group members may request clarification after the initial statement.

The initiator requests advice, coaching, suggestions, brainstorms or names of contact people from other group members.

Other group members respond in turn or all at once if a brainstorm is requested. Notes are taken by the initiator if desired or a request may be made for another to take notes. If the initiator makes a commitment to undertake a particular action as a result of the coaching, he or she will request another member to check at the next meeting whether or not the action took place. The initiator remains in control of the process during his turn.

Ground rules

☐ The initiator is in charge of his time slot. He makes requests to ensure that the time is used in the way he wants.

☐ Other group members aim to empower the initiator. Requests from the initiator are met where possible. Advice is given in the form of suggestions:

   Have you tried . . . ?   I found . . . helpful.   You might like to contact . . . rather than *You must . . . You should . . . I always . . .*

☐ Group members are individually responsible for their own interventions and for not getting tripped up by their own or others' baggage.

☐ The group contracts to meet for a specific number of meetings (say six). At the final meeting, progress is reviewed and a choice made whether or not to continue.

☐ All members commit to be present at all meetings and to be punctual.

Ending
At the completion of the final turn by a group member, there is an opportunity for any final comments or feedback. This will be short, no more than five minutes. The aim is to say anything which will, if not said, add to individual baggage. It is also an opportunity to affirm and encourage one another.

Next meeting
A time and location is confirmed for the next meeting.

For Personal-Development Support Groups

A personal-development support group has as its primary purpose the support and development of each group member. The group may have an outside facilitator who is not there for his own support and personal development. Alternatively, the facilitator may be one of the more experienced members of the support group. Several members may agree to take turns sharing this role.

Note: We do not include a therapy group in our definition of a personal-development support group. A therapy group will be led by one or more therapists who may use facilitation techniques as part of their interaction with the group. Therapists will intervene, both in the content and in the process of the group.

This model is for a group of up to 20 people.

Arrival, environment, ritual
See project group meetings, pages 67-68.

Establishing roles

Clarify or confirm who is facilitating the meeting. An outside facilitator is recommended for a larger group of 15-20. The facilitator checks if other roles—such as recorder and timekeeper—are needed, and assigns roles as necessary by asking for volunteers.

Ground rules

These may include a commitment by each group member to attend every or a certain proportion of meetings. *We commit to attend all meetings for the next six weeks. Each group member will contact the facilitator if an emergency arises.*

Round of sharing

A round of sharing is initiated with an opportunity for each person to speak at some length without interruption. A time limit may be put on this with the agreement of the group—such as three to five minutes depending on the number in the group. Remember that 20 people speaking for three minutes equals 60 minutes. The round may focus on individual progress since the last meeting or on a particular theme—*The highlight of the week for me was . . . .*

Development of issues

The round of sharing may develop a theme or a topic may come up that may then be developed in some depth by the whole group. Alternatively, one or more group members may request individual time to develop their issue and get comment, feedback and coaching from the other group members.

Problem-solving techniques and action methods such as role plays can also be used. A time limit can be negotiated for each person.

Closing round and feedback

A closing round is held in which people either express anything that is still incomplete for them or give affirmations to other members of the group.

Arranging next meeting

Details of the next meeting—facilitator, location, time and theme—are agreed.

Ending

The meeting may end with a ritual which is developed by the group or led by the group members in rotation. Refreshments or informal time may follow.

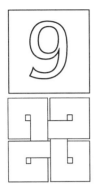

Teamwork, Networking and Large Groups

Teamwork

The model of facilitation we use grew out of the cooperative movement in which the values of equality, shared decision-making, equal opportunity, power-sharing and personal responsibility were considered basic to full cooperation. Our model of facilitation incorporates these values.

The concept of teamwork is often associated with a more hierarchical model. Here a leader such as a manager, coach or supervisor has inspired, trained and organized a group of people into an effective unit. The term *team* is applied to a sports group, where a certain number of players are required, or a *work group*, where interrelated skills are needed to carry out a set of tasks.

Teams tend to be task rather than process-oriented, with socializing together taking the place of process within the group. Group identity can be very strong in a team and can take precedence over individual responsibility and empowerment.

A team often has a team leader or captain who may be appointed by someone other than the team members. Team members may be removed by the team captain, team leader, or coach if they are not performing to the required standard. A manager may gather a team from different work units to complete a specific project. In other cases, a team may be more ongoing and carry out a particular role or set of tasks in a semi-autonomous way.

A team leader or captain may have positional power as well as assigned power. That is, the team leader may be both a manager or supervisor of the team members and also be recognized by team members as taking the leadership role in the team. A team leader who has positional and assigned power will need to operate in a different mode from that of a facilitator.

A facilitator works to maximize equality and power-sharing in a group. A team leader who is also the manager will have constraints in this regard. The team leader must clarify the role and their contract with the team.

A team leader will be involved in both task and process and needs management and leadership skills as well as facilitation skills. However, facilitation skills are designed for cooperative groups. If a team leader has power over group members (such as power to hire and fire or influence promotion) or is personally accountable for team results, some techniques will not be appropriate.

If the team leader or manager desires a more fully cooperative approach to achieve the group purpose, it is preferable to have a team member without positional power facilitate group meetings.

The facilitation role can be rotated between several group members. The team leader will need to clarify exactly what functions and decision-making powers can be delegated to the group and within what constraints. A written contract will be useful.

For team-building and particular sessions requiring maximum input from all team members (planning, evaluation, conflict resolution), the team may choose to bring in an outside facilitator. Professional facilitators can be employed on a freelance basis or through some management consultants.

The committee

The committee is a group based on the democratic principles of one person one vote, majority decision-making, and the value of collective action. Committee rules have now become formalized and institutionalized. The roles of committee chairperson, secretary, and treasurer are usually assigned by the group. Books containing Robert's Rules of Order are readily available from bookstores and libraries.

Networking

Communication between groups for the sharing of information, contacts and other resources is often referred to as *networking*. This term is also used in computing where computers are linked to a common source of information and can communicate with each other. The two meanings are compatible. Networking between groups and individuals is the basis of *community*.

Here we are referring to a physically based community (place) or a community of interest (like-minded people). National and international networks now abound in a wide range of interest group areas. Contact between groups can be in many ways as well as through personal contact and conferences. The telephone, computer links, newsletters, and interest-based magazines are all important means of intergroup contact. Public meetings are a popular means of intergroup contact in physical communities. Conferences are an important means of intergroup contact for national or international interests.

Group-to-group contact is often through representatives or spokespersons—group members who have been assigned the role of speaking for the group on a particular issue. Groups contract with their spokesperson by setting guidelines and limits within which the spokesperson may act.

Groups may have different spokespersons for different types of contact (media, political, financial). Written contact from one group to another may require agreement from the whole group or guidelines and limits for the written material can be set.

Larger groups

Larger groups of between 15 and 30 people tend to operate as a number of formal or informal subgroups as part of the group structure. This is a practical solution so everyone can speak and be heard without undue waiting. In-depth creative work, policy development, and report writing is usually carried out by a subgroup which reports back to the larger group for agreement.

The relationship of subgroups to the larger group needs to be negotiated by the larger group. This negotiation is part of the facilitator's role. As with a spokesperson, clarity is needed to ensure a subgroup acts within the agreed guidelines.

Large group meetings

Large group meetings (more than 30 people and up to several hundred) can be conducted by a chairperson using committee rules or by a facilitator using group facilitation techniques. Large group meetings require skilled facilitation. Part of the meeting may be held in the large group and part in subgroups (workshops/task groups). The size of the subgroups will depend on the number of people at the meeting and the time allowed for feedback to the whole group. If more than eight people, provide a facilitator or ask a subgroup member to take this role. The small groups will usually feed back their discussion and findings to the large group through a spokesperson they have chosen.

The process of a large meeting needs to be planned carefully in advance to ensure the purpose and values are clear and there is opportunity for maximum participation from those attending. A team of facilitators may be used—the main facilitator working with the large group and the assistant facilitators with the subgroups.

Resources such as large electronic whiteboards, large-screen videos, overhead projectors, flip charts, and tables or easels to write on are all useful. Remember to provide name tags, masking tape, pens (whiteboard and felt-tip) and wipers to clean the white boards.

Toolkit

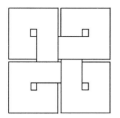

Toolkit

Techniques and Exercises for Developing Group Effectiveness

How to use the toolkit

This part of the book is a toolkit of techniques and exercises for groups to use as a resource. There are a number of ways this resource can be useful.

- ☐ As an introduction to the range of techniques and exercises which are possible in groups.
- ☐ As a guide to specific tools which a group can use.
- ☐ As a basis for creating your own techniques and exercises.
- ☐ As a resource for facilitators to train themselves and develop skills.

Mastery in using this toolkit will come from the practice of choosing or adapting the techniques and exercises to suit the kind of group, its stage of development, the nature of the project and the group mood or energy level. There is no correct technique or exercise. Use the ones that ring true to you.

The toolkit has 18 sections:

A Tools for generating ideas and exploring issues.

B Tools for setting agendas and priorities.

C Feedback tools.

D Tools for the first session of a new group.

E Tools for starting a session.

F Tools for getting clear and handling baggage.

G Tools for speaking and listening.

H Tools for developing trust and group identity.

I Tools for identifying and expressing feelings.

J Tools for affirmation and acknowledgment.

K Tools for visualization and creative thinking.

L Analytic tools.

M Tools for energizing the group.

N Physical contact tools.

O Tools for team-building.

P Tools for resolving conflict.

Q Tools for ending and evaluation.

R Advanced tools.

These sections are somewhat artificial as many techniques could be in several sections. If you are exploring P, Tools for resolving conflict, for example, you will also want to study A, Tools for generating ideas and exploring issues.

Facilitation

All the techniques and exercises require facilitation. Some require experienced facilitation (Advanced tools), while others require little experience (Tools for energizing the group). Reading through the techniques and exercises will give you a sense of the facilitation required. Start with those you feel comfortable with and then begin extending yourself. Most of the exercises are written in the following form:

☐ Purpose
☐ Materials
☐ Time
☐ Process

Purpose

This is to give you an idea of what the exercise is designed for. Many exercises and techniques can be used for a number of purposes and this will become clear as you use them.

Materials

There are some materials needed for all group meetings.
☐ Watch or clock (for monitoring time).
☐ Whiteboard or large sheets of paper. Always have a whiteboard or flipcharts (large sheets of paper)—preferably both. A blackboard is OK. Electronic whiteboards are great if you have access to them as you can make copies of the whiteboard notes as you proceed.
☐ Masking tape and push pins (to attach paper to walls/boards).
☐ Pens and pencils, felt-tips or crayons, whiteboard markers or chalk.
☐ Cloths or eraser (for whiteboard and blackboard).

Other useful resources are:

- ☐ Tissues.
- ☐ Water and glasses.
- ☐ Coffee and tea facilities.
- ☐ Cleaner for the whiteboard. (You'd be amazed how often permanent felt-tip pens are used by accident.)

Time

We have given a time for each exercise, but this is an indication only as it depends on various things like the type of group, the level of group skills, the issues being addressed, and the number of people in the group. Larger groups (over 15) and inexperienced groups will usually require more time.

Process

The process is addressed to the facilitator. Read it carefully before using the exercise. In many cases, it may be helpful to read the process aloud to the group. Begin an exercise by describing the process to the group and seeking agreement to proceed. If there is opposition, provide an opportunity for people to express this and listen for natural apprehension about new ways of doing things. After concerns have been expressed, respond to these and encourage the group to feel the fear and do it anyway. However, don't force a group to do an exercise against its will—the exercise won't work without agreement.

Have fun with these exercises and keep a light touch.

 **A** Tools for Generating Ideas and Exploring Issues

1 Unstructured Rounds

Purpose: To encourage in-depth contribution and sharing.

Materials: Whiteboard (optional).

Time: Variable.

Process: Describe and seek agreement on the process and the focus issue. Each person speaks on the issue without interruption until they have finished. There is no time limit or order of speaking. Other group members listen attentively without responding or commenting. There is only one opportunity to speak.

At the end of the round the facilitator summarizes the range of views, including the main points of similarity and difference, and then checks this with the group. If the aim of the round is to seek agreement, the facilitator may at this stage check out emerging agreements with the group.

To complete the round, agree on and record any follow-up action.

Variations:

☐ Put no limits on the number of times each person can speak.

☐ Follow the round with a general discussion.

☐ The facilitator summarizes the areas of agreement and disagreement and the round continues until agreement is reached.

2 Structured Rounds

Purpose: To encourage participation and ensure that everyone gets the opportunity to be heard on an issue.

Materials: Watch, whiteboard (optional).

Time: The number of group members multiplied by the time allocated for each person (say 1 or 2 minutes each) plus 10 minutes for setting up and completing. For example: 12 people x 2 minutes = 24 minutes + 10 minutes setting up and completing = 34 minutes total time.

This is a basic technique for groups. It can be used as the initial means of exploring an issue or after an issue has been discussed and there is still no clarity. It is useful in conflict resolution because it will bring out the range of views. Rounds enable a group to develop its thinking on an issue. Its power is as a group technique rather than the expression of individual points of view. By hearing everybody's viewpoints, people's thinking can alter, especially if there is more than one round. As with all exercises and techniques, begin by describing the process and getting group agreement.

Process: Clearly identify the issue and focus for the round. It helps to have it written up and displayed. Ask someone to begin, and nominate the direction the round will go. Group members take turns to speak without being interrupted and without response or comment. Other group members give their full attention to the speaker. The timekeeper says when the allocated time is up. If the time is not fully used, the speaker indicates that they have finished and invites the next speaker to start. Group members may say *pass* if they do not wish to contribute.

At the end of the round the facilitator summarizes the range of views, including the main points of similarity and difference, and then checks this with the group.

If the aim is to seek agreement, the facilitator may at this stage check out emerging agreements with the group, saying for example: *I sense the group agrees on these points . . . but needs to clarify these . . .*

It is helpful to write the key words or ideas from each participant on a large sheet of paper or whiteboard as the round progresses. It is also useful to write down the main summary points after the round as part of the summing-up process.

To complete the round, agree on and record any follow-up action. If clarity is not reached after one round, it may be necessary to have a second or third round to see if views have changed or developed.

Note: At first you may need to coach the participants not to interrupt or respond out of turn. You may also need to gently encourage shy members to speak. If several rounds are held, it may be useful to begin with a different person each time.

This is a very simple and powerful technique. Use it often.

3 Brainstorming

Purpose: To generate a large number of ideas quickly and encourage creativity and flexible thinking.

Materials: Watch, whiteboard or large sheet of paper.

Time: Choose a specific time period, say 5 or 10 minutes.

Process: Choose an issue that requires development. Request participants to say whatever idea comes into their heads without censorship and as fast as possible. Write all ideas on the whiteboard. It may be necessary to have two people writing at the same time to catch all the thoughts. Notice how people's thinking is sparked by others' comments and encourage this. Suggest participants be more outrageous. Make sure that people do not evaluate or comment on each other's suggestions. If response is sluggish, get people to stand up or hop on one foot.

Variation: Choose a random factor such as a word from a dictionary opened anywhere, a sound that's just occurred or a color and use this word as a key to generate further brainstorming ideas.

For example: *The issue is restructuring. The random word is yellow. Now use the word yellow to spark ideas related to restructuring.*

4 Subgroups

A useful technique for greater participation in larger groups is to divide them into smaller subgroups. Subgroups may be any number from two to eight people and can be used in a variety of ways.

Pairs: Groups can be divided into pairs to generate ideas, deepen discussion on an issue and raise the group energy level. Example: *Take two minutes to speak to the person next to you about . . .*

When this is complete, ask the pairs if there is anything they want to share with the whole group. Make sure the task and the time limit is clear.

Threes and fours: Groups can be usefully divided into threes and fours to discuss issues and generate alternatives. Small groups provide the opportunity for more participation than is possible in the whole group. It is helpful to have the small group write their findings on a large sheet of paper and agree on a spokesperson. After the allocated time (say 10-15 minutes), have the small groups report their findings to the large group.

More than fours: Larger groups, 15-30, will use subgroups extensively. The subgroups may be up to eight people. Subgroups of five or more will need one of the participants to take on the role of facilitator. Have the subgroups use large sheets of paper for recording ideas and have each subgroup appoint their own spokesperson.

In choosing the number of subgroups take into account the balance between the size of the subgroup and the number of groups required to give feedback to the whole group.

Spokespersons will need five minutes to give feedback. Six groups giving feedback to the whole group is usually about the workable limit. Four is better. A firm time limit needs to be set for both subgroup sessions (no more than 30 minutes) and feedback time by spokespersons.

For larger groups (15-30 people) and large group meetings (more than 30 people) also see Chapter 9.

5 Pros and Cons

Purpose: To clarify the positive and negative aspects of an issue so as to provide a clear framework for choice.

Materials: Two whiteboards or two large sheets of paper.

Time: 15 minutes.

Process: Brainstorm (Tool 3) all the negative aspects of the issue and write them up on one whiteboard. Encourage participants not to hold back and to scrape the bottom of the barrel of negatives. Then stop. You need a clear gap before continuing. You could have participants stand up and stretch. Next, brainstorm all the positive aspects of the issue and write them up on the other whiteboard. Encourage them as before.

Put both lists in front of the group. Ask people to read them silently. At this stage it may be appropriate to ask the group to choose: *Do we go ahead on this issue, or not?*

If a choice is not clear, there are a number of ways of continuing. Use one or a combination of these methods:

1. Have people give their reasons for putting an item on a list and answer any questions.
2. Move into subgroups and discuss all the pros and cons. Have each subgroup choose a course of action and explain that to the group.
3. Identify the critical factors from the list of positives and negatives. Put these in order of priority (see Tool 10). Discuss in subgroups and have them come back to the main group with a recommendation.
4. Choose in the big group whether to proceed on the issue or not and under what conditions.

6 Continuums

Purpose: To explore and visually rank the range of views on any issue.

Materials: None.

Time: 10 minutes to 1 hour, depending on the number of people and depth of discussion wanted.

Process: Create an imaginary line through the room, either corner to corner or the length of the room. One end of the line has a zero-percent (low) ranking and the other, a 100-percent (high) ranking.

Outline the issue and the two extreme positions, one representing zero and one 100 percent. Explain to the participants that this is an intuitive as well as a rational exercise and needs to be approached in a quiet and thoughtful manner.

Have participants walk around to get the feel of the continuum and then place themselves on the line. They may like to try out several positions before putting themselves on the line.

Ask participants to have a conversation with the person on each side of them, explaining why they put themselves in that spot (two minutes per conversation). The people at each end can share with the facilitator, or one another, for their other conversation. Then give people the opportunity to replace themselves on the line.

Invite participants to share with the group their viewpoint and feelings on the issue.

Variations:

☐ Use a slightly curved line so that people can see one another.

- Ask participants at each end of the line to have a public conversation on their reasons for the choice.
- Fold the line in half so that the zero percent and 100 percent ends are together (like folding a bed sheet) and pair up to exchange views. Pairs can then join another pair and share in fours.
- Another dimension can be added by using another axis across the room which can measure such aspects as personal versus public concerns.

Practicing continuums: It is useful and fun to practice using continuums with issues that are not critical to the group. Some suggestions for practice are:

- Birth dates, with January 1 at one end and December 31 at the other.
- Enjoyment of classical music.
- Where you see yourself in terms of physical fitness in the group.
- Where you see yourself in terms of power in the group.
- Satisfaction with progress on the project.

Continuums can also be practiced using controversial issues such as attitudes toward abortion, euthanasia, extraterrestrials, business consolidations and layoffs. Such issues need careful facilitation. The facilitator will need to outline the opposite extremes of the issue and ensure that the environment is safe and accepting.

 **B** Tools for Purposeful Groups

7 Setting Group Objectives

Purpose: To provide the group with a clear focus for action.
Materials: Whiteboard or large sheet of paper and pens.
Time: Variable. At least 1 hour.

Process: Clarify the group vision and purpose (see Tool 54) first, keeping the purpose short and succinct. One sentence is best. Then have the group brainstorm (Tool 3) the main activities or projects which will assist in meeting the group purpose. Write these up so everyone can see them. Have the group agree on the three or four projects which they are the most enthusiastic about and will best achieve the group purpose. Form these into objectives by making each objective **SMART**:

  S pecific
 M easurable
 A ttainable
 R esults oriented (describe a result)
 T imebound (give a clear end date)

We will achieve this result by this date.

For example:

Objective 1: To complete the first draft of the book by March 1.
Objective 2: To have a contract with the publisher signed by June 1.
Objective 3: To have the book announced for publication by the first week of November.

Check that all members of the group are able to commit themselves to attaining these objectives. Is the group able to take responsibility for achieving these objectives or are they outside the control of the group?

Once the objectives have been set, each one will need a written action plan setting out the tasks needed to meet it, with time frames and specific people accountable for each task. The objectives and tasks are then checked regularly at or before the group meetings.

8 Group Values

Purpose: To establish group values.

Materials: Whiteboard.

Time: 30 to 40 minutes.

Process: Brainstorm (see Tool 3) the values that are important to participants regarding the group. Some examples might be:

- ☐ Honesty
- ☐ Confidentiality
- ☐ Punctuality
- ☐ Support
- ☐ Accurate record keeping
- ☐ Acknowledgment
- ☐ Accountability
- ☐ Speed of achieving purpose
- ☐ Friendliness
- ☐ Information sharing
- ☐ Satisfactions

Have the participants rank them in order (see Tool 10). You may then choose to limit the number of values (say to six to ten).

Variation: Have participants choose two or three values which they see as the key values for the group. Then continue the process with Tool 10.

Note: These become the group's values and may be the basis for deciding ground rules.

9 Open Agenda-Setting

(This exercise also appears in Chapter 8, page 70.)

Purpose: To set an agenda for a meeting—often used by groups using consensus decision-making.

Materials: Whiteboard.

Time: 10 minutes.

Process: Each person puts forward the agenda items he or she wants discussed at the meeting and these are listed on the whiteboard so that everyone can see. The name of the person who initiated the agenda item is written next to it.

The initiator is asked by the facilitator to estimate how long it will take to discuss the item and this time is noted next to the item. The facilitator checks this time with the meeting participants and adjusts if a longer time is requested.

If an initiator nominates five minutes or less for other than an information item it is useful to question this, as most items with any discussion at all will take longer. If longer than 30 minutes is requested, this could also be questioned.

The times of all items are added together and the ending time of the meeting checked. If the time needed is longer than the time of the meeting, have a round where each person nominates his or her two most important agenda items. These can be recorded next to the item by marking one check for each person's preferences. This will generate a priority list and items can be addressed in this order. Keep in mind the following:

- ☐ What items must be discussed today.
- ☐ What items are important but not urgent.
- ☐ What items can be left until another meeting or be resolved by another process—for example, delegation to one or two people to decide and act.

10 Priority-Setting

Purpose: To identify priorities after a brainstorm or other similar exercise.

Materials: Brainstorm sheets or lists of previously generated alternatives on a whiteboard.

Time: 10 minutes.

Process: Invite participants to choose two or three preferred ideas or alternatives and note them. It is preferable to have participants write them down individually to avoid influences from other people. Collect the sheets or have people call out their choices.

Mark a check beside each alternative chosen. Add up the checks beside each choice and prioritize accordingly. This priority list can be used as a checklist for further research and development.

Variations:

□ Invite participants to indicate which ideas they prefer and record the number of people who prefer each idea—such as, *Who prefers this alternative?* People may choose as many ideas as they like. Put the number of people who chose against that idea on the list.

□ Invite participants to choose a longer list of preferred ideas, say 10. Have them place these in priority, giving 10 points for the most-preferred down to one for their least-preferred. Collate all the responses (you may need a calculator) and establish your priority order. This variation can take quite a long time to do and to work out.

11 Refining the Priority List

Purpose: To further refine the priority list. This is a complicated process and may need to be used only when expensive alternatives are being considered.

Materials: Whiteboard, calculator.

Time: 30 minutes to 1 hour.

Process: Take each item on the priority list and generate two sublists of advantages or disadvantages. List all the advantages and disadvantages for each alternative and rank each advantage or disadvantage into high, medium and low. Add up the numbers in each category to give a much broader picture. For example: This option has 12 advantages, 6 of which are high, 2 medium and 4 low while it has 23 disadvantages, 13 of which are high, 5 are medium and 5 low.

Reconsider your priority listing in the light of the new information. Check again all high and medium advantages or disadvantages to see if there are any critical factors which could make or break the option as a viable alternative.

 **C** # Feedback Tools

---

12 Practicing Feedback (As a preliminary to giving feedback.)

Purpose: To develop the skills of giving and receiving specific feedback to another person. A practice exercise for Tool 13, Feedback on a Session, Meeting or Project.

Materials: Watch.

Time: 10 minutes.

Process: Have the participants form groups of three. Participants take turns being speaker, listener and observer/timekeeper for two minutes each. Give the speaker a topic such as:

- ☐ Mailboxes
- ☐ My car
- ☐ Photos
- ☐ Camels

- ☐ Childhood
- ☐ Childhood Exotic animals
- ☐ Pins
- *(Make up your own)*

The speaker speaks on the topic for two minutes. The listener gives full attention for the two minutes, then gives detailed specific feedback to the speaker on content and delivery. For example:

You smiled when you spoke about . . . and it added to the story.

Your voice went up at the end of each sentence which gave the impression that all your sentences were questions.

After the feedback, the observer and the speaker comment for one minute on how specific the feedback was.

Rotate the roles, then return to the large group and have participants share what they have learned about giving and receiving feedback.

13 Feedback on a Session, Meeting or Project

Purpose: Giving and receiving specific useful feedback.

Materials: None.

Time: 15 to 30 minutes.

Process: At the end of a session, allow time for feedback. Invite participants to share in two rounds:

1. Things they would like to see changed or improved.
2. Things they appreciated in themselves, others or the whole session, meeting or project.

The rounds can be structured (Tool 2) or unstructured (Tool 1). Do not allow any interruptions, explanations or responses to the feedback. Thank the group for their feedback.

Variation: For inexperienced groups, it may be better to combine the two rounds into one, as it takes a while for people to feel comfortable separating critical feedback from appreciation.

Note: During a large project or workshop, have an interim feedback session or sessions at strategic times, and use the feedback to make changes. Our experience is that it works best to finish with appreciation.

 **D** Tools for the
First Session of a New Group

14 Starting a New Group (For groups of 12 or more)

Purpose: To get the group started and have people meet
and share.

Materials: Watch.

Time: 10 to 30 minutes.

Process: Have the participants walk around the room silently
with no eye contact, paying attention to the physical environment
for about two minutes. Have the participants keep walking and
initiate eye contact with others in the group.

Each person then pairs up with someone he or she doesn't
know but feels comfortable with. Each person in the pair
discusses a topic without interruption for, say, one minute. After
one minute get participants to swap.

Suggested topics:

☐ How did you get here today?
☐ What brought you to this group?
☐ Why did you choose your partner in this exercise?
☐ Where were you born?

Have each pair find another pair they feel comfortable with.
Each person takes a turn to share:

☐ What do you hope to get out of this group?
☐ What are your fears about this group?
☐ What hopes and fears does the group have in common?

Alternatively, topics can relate directly to the purpose of the group or focus on getting to know each other better. For example:

- ☐ Describe your immediate family.
- ☐ What is your living situation at present?
- ☐ What is your favorite drink?

Bring participants back to the whole group. Participants can be asked if they have something to share with the whole group or the exercise can end at this point.

15 Introductions

Purpose: To have each person be seen and heard as a group member.

Materials: Watch.

Time: Number in group times two minutes.

Process: Ask each person to introduce himself or herself by name to the whole group. It may be useful to have each member provide an extra focus by adding one of the following:

- ☐ What brought me to this group.
- ☐ What I want to achieve from this group.
- ☐ What happened before I arrived at this group.
- ☐ My interests.
- ☐ Three places I have lived.
- ☐ Where I would like most of all to be right now.

Suggest a time limit of two minutes per person.

Variation: Ask people to introduce themselves to each other in pairs and then to introduce their partner to the whole group.

Note: If members are going to be introduced to the group by their partner, state this before the paired sharing so people can choose what is to be told to the whole group.

16 Introductions in a Large Group

Purpose: To have each person start to meet others in the group.

Materials: Watch.

Time: 5 to 10 minutes.

Process: Ask everyone to introduce themselves to three people they don't know. Give them a time limit.

Variations:

□ Ask everyone to introduce themselves to three members of the opposite sex.

□ Ask everyone to find someone they don't know and discover their name, where they were from, and one interest they have. Allow, say, two minutes.

17 Build-up Name Game

Purpose: For people to get to know each other's names.
Materials: None.
Time: 10 minutes.

Process: Have one person say his or her own name and the next person says that name and adds his own. Carry this on around the group with each person saying all the previous names and adding his own.

Variations:

☐ Using alliteration, have the round proceed as above but with the addition of a fruit with the same initial letter.
For example.

I am apple Anne.
She is apple Anne and I'm banana Bill.
She is apple Anne, he is banana Bill, and I'm date Dale.

☐ Proceed as above but use qualities group members would like to develop.
☐ As above with a theme, such as picnics, food, people. For example:

I am Anne and I like sandwiches on picnics.
She is Anne and she likes sandwiches, and I am Bill and I like doughnuts on picnics.

18 Name Miming

Purpose: For people to get to know each other's names.
Materials: None.
Time: 20 minutes

Process: Have members take turns miming their names to the group.

19 Throwing Names

Purpose: To remind people of each other's names.
Materials: Ball, cushion or something you can throw.
Time: About 5 minutes.

Process: Have group members stand in a circle and say a person's name before throwing the ball to them. People ask if they can't remember someone's name.

Variation: Add a second ball after, say, one minute.

20 Beginning Ritual

Purpose: To help remind participants why they have come together and to help make the transition from one activity to the next.

Materials: None

Time: About 5 minutes.

Process: The ritual may be a song, prayer, greeting or words of welcome by a senior member of the group or the facilitator. The group may like to make up its own ritual—this will usually be more powerful.

 **E** Tools for Starting a Session

21 Autographs

Purpose: Getting to know each other quickly through sharing.

Materials: A sheet of paper and pencil for each participant.

Time: 10 minutes or until the first person finishes.

FIND SOMEONE WHO	
Wears pajamas	Scratches their nose
Hates cats	Can pat their head and rub their stomach
Can raise one eyebrow	Is a Virgo

Process: Have participants get autographs from others who fit certain descriptions. Each person signs only once. These descriptions can be written on a large sheet of paper or given to each person on a separate sheet. Suggested descriptions:

A person:
Who sings in the shower.
Who has the same pet peeve
   as you.
Who likes jazz.
Who knows a member
   of your family.

Who can't swim.
Who owns a boat.
Who would like to be
   a politician.
Born nearest your birthplace.
Who knows who the Statler
   Brothers are.

The first person to have an autograph for each description is the winner.

22 Meeting People

Purpose: To warm up a group, and for group members to start to get to know each other and share the highs and lows of the week.

Materials: None.

Time: 10 minutes.

Process: Have people walk silently around the room, making eye contact with each other. After a time, have them choose someone with eyes like their own or eyes they like. When everyone is in a pair, have each person share something that has been difficult for them from the past week and then something they are pleased about from the past week.

Variation: Have people walk around the room asking about each other's hobbies. Have them pair up with someone with a hobby similar to theirs, or one they are interested in. When everyone is in a pair, have them share the best thing that has happened to them in the past week.

23 Knots

Purpose: To warm up people to the group.

Materials: None.

Time: 5 minutes.

Process: Have everyone stand up in a circle, shut their eyes and move towards the center until they have found another person's hand with each of their hands. When everyone is holding two hands, have everyone open their eyes and untangle themselves without letting go.

Variation: Have people form two groups. One group starts by holding hands in a circle and then twists itself into a knot. The other group's task is to untwist the knot.

24 Famous Bits and Pieces

Purpose: To warm up a group and to have fun.

Materials: A sheet with the names of well-known people written on it. (If there are 20 in the group, you will need 10 names.) Paper, pens.

Time: 15 minutes.

Process: Ask people to pair up with someone they don't know. Pass around the paper. Have each pair take two minutes to write a list of what their well-known person would have in their pocket, wallet, car glove box or handbag. Collect the lists and pass them out again at random. Display the list of well-known people and ask each pair in turn to guess whose list they have.

Variation: When the lists are completed, have each pair read their list out to the group, with the group attempting to guess the identity of the person.

25 Sharing

Purpose: To have group members share about themselves.

Materials: Large sheet with topics written on it. Suggested topics are:

☐ Your most valued possession.

☐ Your favorite music.

☐ What you are most proud of.

☐ Your pet peeves.

☐ The most fun you've had with your clothes on.

☐ What you would do if you won $1 million.

☐ Two people you would take to Hawaii on vacation.

Time: 10 minutes.

Process: Have the topics displayed prominently and have everyone move around the room. Have people pair up, choose one topic, and share their answer for a minute each. Then have everyone move around the room again and choose another partner for a new topic. Three or four shares is probably enough and creates a good level of energy.

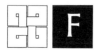 Tools for Getting Clear and
Handling Baggage

26 Starting Clear

Purpose: To enable group members to get clear at the start of a group session.

Materials: None.

Time: 5 minutes.

Process: At the start of a session have participants form pairs and share, for two minutes each way, any concerns or upsets that are uppermost in their minds at the moment, including anything which happened immediately before coming to the group. Encourage participants to share with their partner anything which might get in the way of their being fully present in the group. Then take an imaginary paper bag around to each pair and ask them to mime putting those concerns and upsets into the bag. Tell participants that after the session they can retrieve them on the way out if they want to.

Variations:

☐ As above, but use a real paper bag. Have participants write down key words which symbolize their concerns and put these into the paper bag.

☐ Do this exercise as a visualization. Take the group on a guided fantasy in which the participants take any issues, concerns or upsets to a safe place where they can store them until later.

☐ Paired sharing for two minutes each way on the highs and lows of the past week. Have one person give full attention while the other speaks. Encourage the speakers to express the highs and lows in an exaggerated way, as if they were playing a part. The listener listens very carefully to the concerns without discussion.

27 Where Are You Right Now?

Purpose: To bring people back to the present during a long meeting or workshop, particularly when the energy level is low.

Materials: Watch.

Time: 5 minutes.

Process: Stop the discussion in progress. Have participants move into pairs and share what is happening for them—where they are with the topic and what they want to happen right now. This needs to be brief—one to two minutes each way. Then bring people back to the whole group and see what there is to share.

Variation: Stop the discussion. Have a round addressing the question: *What is going on for you right now?* Ask people to be brief, no more than about one minute each. This avoids long stories about situations rather than the direct expression of thoughts and feelings.

28 Identifying Baggage

Purpose: To identify our own baggage.

Materials: Watch, large sheet of paper for each participant, plus either crayons, felt pens, paints or pastels, in a range of colors.

Time: 1 hour.

Process: Introduce the ideas in this book relating to baggage and being present in the group. Have each person draw a big bag taking up most of the sheet of paper. In the bag have them write and draw their fears, hopes, dreams, desires and hang-ups. Give time for each topic. Encourage a quiet reflective atmosphere. Total time 15 minutes. Then have each person pair up with someone they don't know well and share their drawing. Allow 10 minutes. Next, put all the drawings on display for participants to walk around and look at. Allow 5 minutes. Finally, come back to the whole group and have a discussion on what people noticed.

29 Strongly Held Beliefs

Purpose: To identify and share strongly held beliefs.

Materials: Pens and paper plus large sheet of paper or whiteboard.

Time: 1 hour

Process: Have participants write down their strongly held beliefs on a sheet of paper. Give an area of focus to the group such as work, play, babies, bosses, computers, sports. Have a round in the whole group with each person sharing their beliefs. Ask participants to note on their paper any of their beliefs which are shared by others. At the end of the round, develop a list (on the large sheet of paper) of beliefs which are held by more than one person in the group and note the number of people with that belief. Are there any beliefs shared by the whole group?

Variation: Start with a group discussion on a topic. Encourage people to express their different beliefs. After 10 minutes stop the discussion. Then have participants write down their strongly held beliefs (and continue above process). In the sharing round ask participants to share how they felt when people expressed beliefs different from themselves. Did any one get annoyed or upset? Why was this?

30 Sharing Withholds

Purpose: To free up energy and clear a space in the baggage for the group to be in relationship.

Materials: None.

Time: 10 minutes to 1 hour, depending on the development of the group.

Process: Have a round in which each person shares something they have been withholding from the group—that is, something they have been thinking but not saying. Withholds usually have to do with judgments and assessments about ourselves, others or what the group is doing. The facilitator can assist by suggesting a starting phrase:

> *I would contribute more to the group if . . .*
> *You would understand me more if you knew that . . .*
> *Sometimes I . . . (describe behavior) when I feel . . . (the feeling).*
> *If I could wave my magic wand and alter one thing in the group right now, it would be . . .*

This exercise works best when the round is continued several times (usually three) until people feel brave enough to share what they are *really* withholding.

Note: Lack of energy usually has to do with withholding—that is, failure to communicate. We are alive to the extent that we are prepared to communicate. Remember that we withhold out of fear, and the group climate needs to be one of trust and generous listening for participants to share their withholds. The more pressing the withhold, the scarier it is to share it. There needs to be a level of trust in the group for this exercise to be effective. If you are not sure, practice some trust-building exercises first.

31 Upset on Arrival

Purpose: To attend to anyone who is upset on arrival at a meeting.

Materials: None.

Time: 5 minutes.

Process: If someone comes to a group very upset, this needs to be acknowledged as soon as possible. It is preferable to handle it before the meeting. If it is a work group, ask the participant if there is something they need to attend to before they join the group or if they would prefer not to attend the meeting. A very upset person may distract everybody from concentrating on the business of the meeting. Sometimes it may be sufficient just to acknowledge the participant's upset and remind them of the purpose of the group.

If it is a support group, seek agreement at the beginning of the group for this person to have some group time as soon as possible. Allow the participant to share his or her upset with as little comment from others as possible. Ask the participant if he or she has any requests of the group. Encourage him or her to form the needs into a specific request, for example:

I would like to sit by Anne and support her.
I would like to make a phone call to Bill now and then return to the group.

Don't allow the group to get into long discussions, advice-giving or commiserations. Take the attitude that each participant is a healthy, self-generating adult. If a participant is often upset or distressed on arrival at the group, it may be advisable to suggest privately that he or she seek individual assistance such as support or counseling.

G Tools for Speaking and Listening

32 Free Attention 1

Purpose: To practice being present to another person.
Materials: Watch.
Time: 10 to 30 minutes.

Process: Have group members sit facing one another in pairs. Get them to initiate eye contact with each other for five minutes. This time can be extended, after practice, to 15 or 20 minutes. During the exercise, ask an occasional question like: *Are you present to your partner or have you drifted off somewhere?* or *Do you have enough attention to meet, and be present for your partner?* After the time is up, invite partners to share their experience verbally with one another.

Note: This exercise gives practice in giving another person non-judgmental, encouraging, free attention. Free attention is all the available awareness that is not distracted by the immediate environment or caught up in internal tensions.

33 Free Attention 2

Purpose: To practice being present to another person.
Materials: Watch.
Time: 10 to 30 minutes.

Process: Have group members sit facing one another in pairs. Get them to make eye contact for about five minutes. Have one person speak on a selected topic while the other gives free attention. Suggested topics are:

- ☐ Houses I have lived in.
- ☐ A game I played as a child.
- ☐ My favorite car.
- ☐ My favorite meal.
  (Make up other topics)

After three minutes, ask the participants to swap roles. Have the participants share in pairs and then in the whole group.

34 Encouraging Contribution

Purpose: To encourage shy or noncommunicative people to share and take an active part in the group.

Materials: Five tokens (such as matches, coins or shells) per participant.

Time: This exercise is designed to be used as part of a meeting. It will take five minutes to explain and 10 minutes to debrief at the end.

Process: The facilitator (or group member) acts as an initial holder of all the tokens. Each time a participant speaks, give them one token (up to five per person). Participants without five tokens at the end of the meeting will be allocated tasks—putting the chairs and other items away, doing the dishes.

Note: The mood of this exercise needs to be light and encouraging. When quiet participants are given tokens, group members can be encouraged to acknowledge their contribution.

Debrief: Encourage the participants to share how they felt about the number of tokens they ended up with.

Variation: At the beginning of the meeting, everyone gets five tokens. Each time they contribute they hand one back. People left with tokens at the end of the meeting are encouraged to identify when they could have used them.

35 Anti-rambling Device

Purpose: To educate participants to take responsibility for letting others know when they are day-dreaming or getting bored.

Materials: None.

Time: This is designed to be used as part of a meeting and will take five minutes to explain and 10 minutes to debrief at the end.

Process: Choose a signal—for example, tugging on ear, hands over ears, a stop signal by making the hands into a T. Participants must use the signal at least five times each during the meeting to avoid being penalized. The signal is to be used when participants realize their minds are wandering or they are feeling bored. Participants who don't use up all their signals will be allocated tasks at the end of the meeting—putting the chairs and other items away, doing the dishes.

Note: People have a reluctance to draw attention to other people's annoying behaviors. The use of a penalty helps break through this resistance. After several practices, ask participants to use the signal when needed at any time.

Debrief: Encourage the participants to share how they felt when confronted by the signal and when using the signal.

Variation: At the beginning of the meeting, everyone gets five tokens. Each time they signal, they hand one back. People left with tokens at the end of the meeting are encouraged to identify when they *could* have used them.

36 Building a Communication Web

Purpose: To demonstrate group interaction and participation.

Materials: A ball of yarn or string.

Time: 20 minutes.

Process: Nominate a topic of discussion while holding the end of the ball of yarn. When the next person speaks, throw them the ball of yarn, while still holding on to your end. The ball is passed or thrown from participant to participant as the discussion continues. When the discussion ends, invite the group to look at, and comment on, the patterns of group interaction and participation as shown by the yarn.

37 Speaking Distance

Purpose: To demonstrate the effect of body position and nonverbal behavior on communication. To identify personal space needs.

Materials: None.

Time: 5 minutes.

Process: Have the participants pair up and choose one to be A and one to be B. The pairs stand face to face, close to each other and have a conversation for a minute. Then B moves gradually away from A while the conversation continues for another minute until they are four to five yards apart. Have the pairs share with each other the effect the different distances had on the conversation. Then bring the pairs back to the whole group for sharing.

Variations:

- ☐ B moves from side to side.
- ☐ B sits down facing A.
- ☐ B moves behind A.
- ☐ B looks away from A.
- ☐ B fiddles with something while talking.
- ☐ B puts feet apart and hands on hips.
- ☐ A and B stand approximately three yards apart. While they converse, B moves gradually toward A until A feels uncomfortable, at which point A says *Stop!* Share with the whole group as in the main exercise.

38 My Most Precious Possession

Purpose: To deepen group relationships through sharing.

Materials: Pens, crayons, felt pens of different colors, and paper.

Time: Drawing time (about 10 minutes) plus five minutes per group member.

Process: Participants draw a picture of their most precious possession. This may be a person or an object. Participants then sit in the middle of the group and describe their precious possession. Other members listen attentively without speaking.

Note: This can be a very powerful exercise and often brings up strong feelings for all participants. It is particularly useful for family groups as children enjoy it.

Variations:

- ☐ This exercise can be done without drawing by having participants tell the group about their most precious possession.
- ☐ It can also be done by having each person bring a treasured item, or a photograph of someone or something that is treasured.

39 Flowering

Purpose: Getting to know each other, creating a relaxed feeling in the group and encouraging self-confidence.

Materials: Prepared worksheet (see diagram) and pens.

Time: 30 to 60 minutes depending on the size of the group.

Process: Have participants fill out the worksheet, working quietly on their own. Allow time for everyone to complete their sheet. After 10 minutes invite participants to move around the room and talk with others about their flowers. If participants are staying with one person for more than two or three minutes, encourage them to move on. Have participants return to the whole group. Invite sharing and comments.

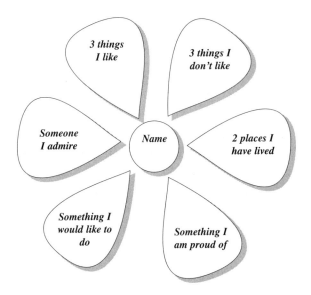

40 If You Were a . . .

Purpose: Building trust and encouraging creative thinking.

Materials: None.

Time: 10 to 15 minutes.

Process: Have one person in the group be the focus of attention. In the form of a round, each member is to describe that person as if the person were an object. For example: *If Bill were a car, he would be a red MG.* When each person has described Bill, have the next person be the focus. Other suggested categories are:

☐ Book
☐ Tree
☐ Building
☐ Job
☐ Recording
☐ Piece of music
☐ Machine
   (Make up more as required)

Variations:

☐ Use a different category for each person.
☐ Have people describe themselves as a car, building etc.
☐ Have person A describe person B as a car, then B describes C as a car. Continue until everybody has been described.

41 Quality Weaving

Purpose: To strengthen group trust and encourage self-recognition.

Materials: Lots of different colored yarn to be cut into equal lengths of about two feet, scissors.

Time: 30 minutes.

Process: Invite each participant to think of three qualities they would like to possess. Have them choose a different colored length of yarn to represent each quality. In silence have the participants braid the qualities together. Invite them to reflect on weaving these qualities into their lives. Then have participants sit in a circle and invite each to share the qualities they have claimed. After each person has shared, invite them to place their woven band around their forehead.

42 Mirroring

Purpose: To practice being present with one or more people.

Materials: Watch.

Time: 5 to 15 minutes.

Process: Have participants work in pairs facing one another an arm's length apart. Have them make eye contact and have one person, A, begin to move their body slowly using their arms, torso, shoulders, head, etc. The other person in the pair, B, begins to mirror the movement. After one or two minutes call *Change* and B becomes the movement leader with A mirroring. Remind participants to maintain eye contact. Call *Change* several times. Have participants return to the whole group and share what they got out of the exercise.

Variations:

- ☐ This exercise can be repeated with different partners, to music, to poetry and in threes, fours, or larger groups.
- ☐ It can also be done as a contact exercise where palms are touching.
- ☐ Add the instruction: *Continue mirroring with no leader.*

43 Windows

Purpose: To get to know each other better.

Materials: Paper and pens.

Time: 30 minutes.

Process: Give each participant a sheet of paper and have them fold it in into quarters. In each quarter (window) participants write their responses. Ask them to write four of the following (or make up your own):

- ☐ Three things you do well.
- ☐ Three things you enjoy.
- ☐ A pet peeve.
- ☐ Somewhere you'd rather be.
- ☐ A goal you have set for the next six months.
- ☐ Your favorite food/color/season etc.

Have the participants share in pairs, preferably with someone they don't know well. Bring the participants back to the large group and invite them to share something from one of the categories.

44 Fairy Tales

Purpose: To identify some of our life myths.

Materials: Paper and pens.

Time: Up to 1 hour.

Process: Ask participants to choose their favorite fairy tale and write the name of it down. Ask them to write down the main characters. Ask them which character they identify with most closely. Have them spend five minutes in silence considering how they have lived out this character in their lives. Have them write a few notes and insights about this.

Next, have participants choose another person with whom to share their thoughts and insights for five minutes each way. Reform the whole group and invite participants to share these tales and how they have lived out the characters in their lives.

45 Find the Identity

Purpose: For participants to reveal and describe themselves.

Materials: Pencil and paper for each participant.

Time: 20 to 30 minutes.

Process: Have each person write four or five adjectives or phrases to describe himself or herself. Collect the sheets and hand them out randomly. Each person reads the sheet he or she has been given and attempts to find its owner. Come back to the whole group and share about the exercise.

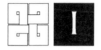 **I** # Tools for Identifying and Expressing Feelings

46 Expressing Feelings

Purpose: To expand awareness and to encourage expression of feelings.

Materials: Strips of card or paper 5 x 7 inches with the beginnings of sentences written on them. Examples are:

- ☐ I felt happy when . . .
- ☐ I was sad when . . .
- ☐ What energizes me is . . .
- ☐ What I enjoy is . . .
- ☐ What I get angry about is . . .
- ☐ I dislike . . .
- ☐ I laugh at . . .
- ☐ The last time I remember being frightened was . . .
  (Make up your own)

Time: 20 minutes.

Process: Divide the group into groups of three to five people. Give each group a number of the cards face down. Have one person take the top card and ask another person to complete the question. After doing so, that person takes the cards and asks the next person to complete the next sentence. When all the sentences have been completed at least once, get participants to return to the whole group and share what they got out of the exercise.

47 Thoughts versus Feelings

Purpose: To identify the difference between thoughts and feelings. (Many people have difficulty in making this distinction and when asked how they feel, respond with a thought.)

Materials: Handout sheets for each pair, and pens. The handout sheet has the following written on it:

☐ This meeting is going on too long.
☐ I'm sick of people saying they're too busy.
☐ I feel we should go on to the next topic.
☐ I'd like to change the room around.
☐ You look great in those clothes.
☐ I'm sorry you are leaving.
☐ We never seem to get anywhere.
   (Add others)

Time: 30 minutes.

Process: Divide the group into pairs. Give each pair a handout. Ask the pairs to discuss which of the statements are thoughts and which are feelings. Allow 10 minutes. Bring participants back to the whole group and discuss each statement in turn.

48 Feelings Continuum

Purpose: To physically show the range of feelings on any topic and open it up for discussion.

Materials: None.

Time: From 5 to 30 minutes or more.

Process: Define a curved line in the room, with one end being an extremely positive feeling and the other being an extremely negative feeling. Ask people to place themselves along the continuum according to how they feel about the topic. Examples of topics are:

- ☐ How well you feel you are supported in your work.
- ☐ How well you feel you are listened to in the group.
- ☐ How you feel about a certain holiday.

Invite people to share with someone near them on the continuum and then in the whole group.

J Tools for Affirmation and Acknowledgment

49 Affirmations and Acknowledgments

Purpose: Giving and accepting acknowledgment.

Materials: Watch.

Time: 10 minutes.

Process: Have participants pair up with someone they know and share for two minutes each way what they appreciate about each other. After each acknowledgment the listener says *Thank you* but makes no other comment. Have participants repeat the process with someone they don't know well.

Variations:

☐ Have participants repeat the process with everyone in the group.

☐ Use a specific focus such as:

Contribution toward the project.
Personal qualities.
Participation in the group.
Leadership.

50 Gifts

Purpose: To have the group imaginatively express appreciation of each other.

Materials: None.

Time: 20 to 30 minutes.

Process: Have participants stand or sit in a circle. Ask participants to mentally choose someone in the group they wish to acknowledge. Invite participants in turn to go up to this person, holding an imaginary present in their hands and say: *I am giving you this gift of a . . . in appreciation of . . .* Continue until everyone has received at least one present.

51 Positive Messages

Purpose: To promote trust in the group.

Materials: Paper and pens.

Time: 30 minutes.

Process: Distribute a piece of paper to each group member. Ask each person to write a positive message about the group and the experience of working with the other group members. Collect the papers and shuffle them. Redistribute them. Ask each participant to read aloud the paper they have received.

52 Written Feedback

Purpose: To encourage acknowledgment and feedback and to have a written record of this.

Materials: Paper, pens and pins.

Time: 30 minutes.

Process: Have participants pin a piece of paper to their backs, then invite them to write positive comments on each other's sheets. After time has been allowed for everyone to write their comments, the sheets are given to their owners. Some participants may like to share. Participants are requested to take their sheets home and pin them up in a prominent place where they will see them often.

This is a very powerful exercise. It is most useful for a group which has been together for some time. Do not attempt this exercise until you are sure the group is able to distinguish between positive feedback and veiled criticism.

K Tools for Visualization and Creative Thinking

53 Relaxation and Preparation for Visualization

Purpose: To relax group members and form a basis for self-disclosure, healing and problem-solving.

Materials: Comfortable chairs or carpet to lie on.

Time: 15 minutes.

Process: Have participants get comfortable sitting or lying down. Have them close their eyes and start being aware of their breathing. Invite them to relax on each exhalation. *Each time you breathe out, relax, relax a little more.* If there are any outside noises, acknowledge them and have the participants include them in the process.

Invite participants to relax and allow the relaxation to spread and flow through their entire body. Invite them to find a part of their body which is not relaxed and imagine those specific muscles relaxing. Alternatively, have them exaggerate the tension in the tight parts of their body and then relax. You can work through all the major muscle groups starting at the toes and working up to the top of the head.

Invite the participants to thank their bodies for being as relaxed as they are.

54 Building the Group Vision

Purpose: To develop a common vision and purpose for the group.

Materials: Large sheets of paper.

Time: Variable, about 1 hour.

Process: Start with Tool 53, Relaxation and Preparation for Visualization. When people are relaxed, ask them to project their thoughts forward in time to the successful realization of their dreams of the group (or organization). Perhaps they have been on a space trip for x years (the expected life of the group) and have now been returned to earth. The spaceship returns them to the place where the group projects have taken place. The projects have been outstandingly successful.

Using the technique of an Unstructured Round (Tool 1), ask each person to describe what they see (also touch, hear, smell or taste) as they move around the physical area. Encourage each person to be specific. *Look carefully. What do you see? Hear? Smell?* etc.

Write down the key words and phrases from each person on large sheets of paper and pin them where everyone can see. At the end of the round, ask if there are any further contributions. The group may be so inspired they would like another round.

When the process is completed, encourage the group to own the whole vision as the group vision. If there is strong disagreement to some parts of the vision, identify the common areas and differences. Then ask the group to develop an inspiring sentence which encapsulates the essence of the vision. Keep this short and punchy (12 words or less so that everyone can remember it easily). This sentence is the purpose or mission of the group. Refer back to it often and display it in prominent places for your group to be constantly reminded of it.

55 Contributing to the Group Project

Purpose: To identify what each person will contribute to the project.

Materials: Large sheet of paper and colored pens.

Time: 5 minutes.

Process: Start with Tool 53, Relaxation and Preparation for Visualization. Then take participants on a guided fantasy to discover what they can contribute or bring to the group project. Make up your own guided fantasy. This could include taking participants to a favorite place, or down a cave, along a beach, by a lake, into another dimension, on a rocket trip. Make sure your fantasy is consistent, flowing and gentle in nature. It's probably not a good idea to have the rocket crash on Mars because you may lose some of your participants for the rest of the exercise.

When you have taken the participants to a fantasy destination, invite them to find an imaginary object which symbolizes their contribution to the project and have them bring it back with them. After guiding them back to the present, invite them to share by describing or drawing their object and what it represents in terms of their contribution to the project. Each object could be drawn on a large sheet of paper which could be kept as a record and reminder of what people are contributing.

56 Personal Perspectives

Purpose: A reflective and fun exercise to help focus attention inward. It can be used at the end of a busy working session or during a day workshop to alter the energy level.

Materials: Paper and pens.

Time: 20 minutes.

Process: Assure participants before the exercise that there will be no requirement to share their responses with others.

1. Invite participants to choose their favorite animal and write it down, followed by three adjectives which describe the animal. For example—horse: swift, powerful, majestic.
2. Have each participant choose their second favorite animal and write it down, followed by three adjectives which describe it.
3. Have participants imagine themselves in the depths of a tropical jungle surrounded by lush vegetation. High above a shaft of light pierces the high canopy and shines down to the jungle floor. Have participants put themselves in the scene and write down three adjectives describing how they feel.
4. Have participants imagine themselves alone on a beach at sunset and write down three adjectives describing their feelings.
5. Have participants imagine themselves in a room with white walls, white floor, white ceiling, and no doors, no windows and no furniture. They are seated on the floor looking at one wall. There is a nail driven into the wall. Have them describe how they are feeling with three adjectives.

Then explain that an interesting and useful way of interpreting their responses is as follows:

1. The first set of adjectives are about themselves—how they are.
2. The second set describes their ideal partner.
3. The third set describes their sexuality.
4. The fourth set describes their spirituality.
5. The fifth set describes their death.

Do not request any sharing. Participants may volunteer to share if they want to.

No 57 Group Fantasy

Purpose: To develop group identity and alignment.

Materials: None.

Time: 15 to 30 minutes.

Process: Have everyone get into a comfortable position and relax their breathing. Say: *Each time you breathe out, relax; relax a little more.* Repeat similar phrases as required. After a few minutes suggest a theme for a group fantasy such as:

- ☐ My ideal house.
- ☐ My ideal vacation.
- ☐ My ideal working environment.

Invite each person in turn to describe, out loud, aspects of the theme so that a picture is built up for the group. Keep going until everyone has had one or two turns. At the end of the exercise, ask the participants: *Is there anything you want to share about doing that exercise?*

58 Mind Expander

Purpose: To develop group identity and expand the mind.

Materials: None.

Time: Up to 30 minutes.

Process: Invite participants to sit comfortably and relax their breathing. Suggest that they allow their minds to stretch sideways. Invite participants to respond verbally to each of the following questions in their own time. Allow several minutes for each question. Suggested questions are:

☐ What is the color of soft?
☐ What is the smell of blue?
☐ What is the sound of fur?
☐ What is the taste of happiness?
☐ What is the feel of music?
☐ What does warm sound like?
(Have fun making up your own)

After the exercise ask the question: *Is there anything you'd like to share about that exercise?*

 **L** Analytic Tools

59 Mapping Your Family, Friends and Networks

Purpose: Recognizing relationships. Deepening group relationships through sharing.

Materials: A large sheet of paper for each person plus colored pens, crayons or paint. Masking tape or some method of attaching the sheets to the wall.

Time: 1 hour.

Process: Have each participant take a large sheet of paper and draw himself or herself in the center of the page. A circle with his or her name will be sufficient. Using the colors they are attracted to, have the participants draw in family members, friends and networks. Draw the links between people and groups. If this is a work-related workshop, ask participants to draw in their colleagues, coworkers and networks. Allow 10 to 15 minutes.

Have participants stick their sheets to the wall to create a gallery. Then ask participants to walk around and look at one another's maps. Finally, bring participants back to the whole group and ask them the following questions:

☐ *What did you notice about the maps?*
☐ *What did you learn from your own map?*
☐ *What did you learn from other people's maps?*
☐ *How do the maps complement one another?*
☐ *How do the maps differ from one another?*
☐ *How do your networks overlap?*

60 Mapping Leadership

Purpose: To identify where leadership lies in a group.

Materials: Large sheets of paper and pens.

Time: 40 minutes.

Process: Have each participant draw the groups they are involved in on a large sheet of paper. Each can be represented by a circle or some other symbol and is named. Ask people to identify the key roles in each group—for example, chairperson, facilitator, team leader, secretary, recorder, timekeeper, treasurer. Then have participants consider each group in turn and identify where leadership is in the group. Have them consider the following questions:

- *Does leadership lie with people who have defined roles or does it lie with other group members?*
- *Does the leadership role vary from time to time and on what basis?*
- *Are there hidden leaders in the group who lead through supporting or empowering others? Who never shows up as a leader?*
- *What could be a reason for this?*
- *How could each person in the group be empowered to take a leadership role? Which leaders do you support?*
- *What is their leadership style?*
- *Which leaders to you resist supporting, or even subvert at times?*

Have participants move into twos or threes to share their insights. After eight to 10 minutes invite them back into the large group for sharing.

61 Mapping Power

Purpose: To identify where power lies in a group and to identify different kinds of power.

Materials: Large sheets of paper and colored pens.

Time: 30 minutes.

Process: Have each participant draw the groups they are involved in on a large sheet of paper. Each can be represented by a circle or some other symbol and is named. Ask people to identify the key roles in each group—for example, chairperson, facilitator, team leader, secretary, recorder, timekeeper, treasurer. Then have participants identify where the different kinds of power are in the groups:

- ☐ Positional power
- ☐ Assigned power
- ☐ Knowledge power
- ☐ Personal power
- ☐ Factional power

Take each kind of power in turn and read aloud the descriptions in Chapter 2, pages 10-12. Have participants write down the person or persons who have the different kinds of power in each group. After addressing each of the five power types, have participants consider the following questions:

- ☐ *What patterns do you see?*
- ☐ *Do people with positional power also have assigned power?*
- ☐ *Does this increase their power?*
- ☐ *Are there people in your group who have three or four kinds of power?*

☐ *What are your feelings or thoughts about these people?*
☐ *What kinds of power do you have?*
☐ *Do you have the same kinds of power in each group?*
☐ *Are there any groups where you have no power?*
☐ *How could you become more powerful in this group?*
☐ *Are you more comfortable with your own power or someone else's?*
☐ *Do you avoid assigned and positional power?*

Have participants move into twos or threes to share their insights. After eight to 10 minutes invite them back into the large group for sharing.

62 Planning

Note: This is a general planning exercise for all kinds of groups. For specific project groups, such as work-based project teams, a more rigorous process of setting goals, specific objectives and measurable results is needed.

Purpose: To identify the issues to be addressed and actions to be taken to achieve the group purpose.

Materials: Pens and paper for everyone, sheets of paper and felt pens.

Time: 40 to 60 minutes.

Process: State clearly the purpose of the meeting or sessions. Write this on the whiteboard and check that everyone is in agreement.

The group purpose is to . . .

If there is not full agreement, it needs to be resolved now. Use a technique such as rounds (Tools 1 and 2).

In pairs get people to think about the purpose and write down the issues and tasks involved. Now move into subgroups of four, and have them reach consensus on the top five issues and tasks and record them on large sheets. Come back to the whole group and compare the issues and tasks of each subgroup.

Discuss and generate a master list of main issues and tasks. These become the agenda for the meeting or sessions.

 Tools for Energizing the Group

63 Naughty Words

Purpose: To lift the group energy level.

Materials: None.

Time: 5 seconds.

Process: When energy is becoming very low in a group, perhaps after a meal, and people are not concentrating or are dozing off, add something outrageous into your conversation, spoken in a normal voice. For example, drop the word *sex* into the conversation. Usually everyone wakes up immediately. If people are very sleepy you may need to be a little more imaginative. For example:

The difficulty with this business plan is that we have a lack of information and statistics and also as I had sex for six hours last night, I have difficulty in concentrating on the calculations of the budget forecast.

At the very least you'll know who is awake after this.

64 Physical Energizers

Here are a variety of exercises to try:

- ☐ Have the group stand up and stretch.
- ☐ Do jumping jacks.
- ☐ Throw a ball round the group. Throw two or three balls around the group at the same time.
- ☐ Cross-body touching. Elbow to opposite knee 20 times, fast.
- ☐ Rapid tapping with three fingers on the breastbone.
- ☐ Tap head and rub stomach simultaneously, then swap movements.

In pairs, one person bends forward while the other taps them with fingertips from the top of the head down their back, buttocks and legs. Then swap over.

65 Mental Energizers

Some suggestions to raise the mental energy of the group:

☐ Riddles
☐ Limericks
☐ Quick puzzles
☐ Brain-teasers
☐ Jokes
☐ Songs

66 I'm Going on a Journey

Purpose: A frustrating game to raise the energy of the group.
Materials: None.
Time: 20 minutes

Process: Explain to the participants that this is a light-hearted game. If they take it too seriously this game can cause some upset, particularly among members of the group who consider themselves to be intelligent.

Have participants sit in a circle. Begin the game by saying: *I'm going on a journey to the moon and I'm taking* . . . Complete with an object whose name begins with the first letter of your first name. (That is the code, but you don't tell them what it is.) For example, Bill says: *I'm going on a journey to the moon and I'm taking some butter.* Go on: *I'd love you all to come with me, but there's limited space on the rocket. I'll decide whether you can come depending on what you bring.*

Then continue as a round and tell each person they can come or not depending on whether they use the code of bringing an object which starts with the same initial letter as their first name. Don't explain the code at any stage.

Variation: Make up another code, such as an item of clothing worn by the person on the immediate right of the speaker.

67 Changing Positions

Purpose: To energize a group by encouraging people to change places.

Materials: None.

Time: 5 minutes.

Process: When you notice that participants always sit in the same place, ask them to swap places. This can be done before a break so that members come back to different seats afterwards. After swapping, invite people to share in pairs about how they feel about swapping places, or alternatively about something entirely different—for example, something great that has happened to them in the past week—for about one minute each way.

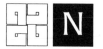

68 Massage

Purpose: To relax group members and build trust.

Materials: Massage oil can be used, but is not necessary.

Time: 10 minutes.

Process: Have participants get into pairs. Have each pair take it in turn to massage each other's feet or hands for five minutes. Some participants may find this exercise a problem if it is the end of the day and their feet are smelly. It may be helpful if there is somewhere to wash and dry the feet before the exercise.

Variations:

- ☐ Participants massage each other's feet at the same time.
- ☐ Participants can also massage each other's heads, or upper backs, either for five minutes each way, or simultaneously.

The head or back massage can also be done in a circle, with each participant sitting or standing close to the person in front and all facing one way around the circle. Each participant massages the head of the person in front. It is also fun to do this massage on the floor with each person seated between the legs of the person behind.

Another variation has the participants standing in a tight circle and then all sitting simultaneously on to the knees of the person behind. A head or back massage can be done if the participants can keep their balance.

69 Group Sculpture

Purpose: To build trust, intimacy and awareness of others.

Materials: None.

Time: 30 minutes.

Process: Have participants move into pairs. Have them choose one person to be sculptor and one to be the sculpture. The sculptor gently moves the other's body into a sculpture using their imagination. The sculpture allows their body to be moved and remain where the sculptor places it. The exercise is done in silence or to music. The participants do not speak. After five minutes, the participants swap roles.

The next part of the exercise is to create a group sculpture. One or two participants take the role of sculptor while the others become part of the sculpture. The sculptors move the participants into a group sculpture, making sure that individuals can keep their balance. The mood of the exercise is gentle and slow with the sculptors and participants being very aware of one another. After the first group sculpture, which can take five minutes, create another with different sculptors.

At the end of the exercise, invite participants to share.

70 Boston Lap Game

Purpose: A fun game involving physical contact. It can be done with very large groups—it takes its name from the fact that it was once done by 1,700 people in a stadium in Boston.

Materials: None.

Time: 10 minutes.

Process: Have the participants stand in a circle with shoulders almost touching. Each turns to the left so they are directly behind someone. As the facilitator counts to three, participants slowly lower themselves to sit on to the knees of the person behind them while holding the waist of the person in front. The number three is the signal for the moment of sitting. Poor timing can send the whole group to the floor. If at first you don't succeed, try again. It's fun. Have everyone do the counting this time.

Note: Suggest those with bad knees may like to sit (or stand) this one out.

71 Curl-up Hug

Purpose: To develop group intimacy.

Materials: None.

Time: 10 minutes.

Process: Have participants stand in a line, side by side, holding hands. A person at one end curls in towards the line and the rest of the group gradually forms a spiral as they keep turning.

Variation: Have the group gather around one person and have a group hug with him or her in the middle. This is particularly useful if the group wants to give a member special attention—for example, when it's his or her birthday or if the person has had something bad happen to him or her.

72 Wizards, Gnomes and Giants

Purpose: A fun game with lots of hilarity.

Materials: None.

Time: 15 minutes.

Process: This is a version of stone, scissors, paper. Form two teams facing one another. For each action the teams will first need to form a huddle and choose what to be of the following three characters:

- ☐ *Wizards* who stretch their hands out in front, wiggle their fingers and make a *whoooooooo* sound.
- ☐ *Giants* who put their hand up above their heads, jump up and down and make a low *ho-ho-ho* sound.
- ☐ *Gnomes* who get down close to the ground with their hands by their ears and make a high *ning-ning-ning* sound.

Tell the participants that wizards win over giants, giants win over gnomes, and gnomes win over wizards. Teams line up facing each other, about two yards apart, with each having a safe zone behind, say, the wall. The facilitator starts each action off by saying: *One, two, three, go.* Each team then acts out its chosen character and the winners chase the other team to tag them before they reach the safety zone. Anyone tagged before reaching the safety zone joins the winning team. If teams both choose the same character, nothing happens (except hilarity).

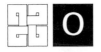 Tools for Team-building

73 Flip the Frisbee

Purpose: A fun game to help develop cooperation among team members.

Materials: Frisbee®, or book of similar size.

Time: 10 minutes.

Process: Have participants get on their hands and knees in a circle with their heads towards the center. Place a Frisbee on the back of a participant, who then has to pass it on to the back of the next person by flipping it from their back. Continue round the group.

Variation: This can be done as a competition between teams, each using a Frisbee.

74 Pass the Balloon

Purpose: A fun game to help develop cooperation among team members.

Materials: Balloon.

Time: 10 minutes.

Process: Have participants stand in a circle and have one person hold the balloon under their neck. It is then passed on to the next group member without using hands, until it goes all the way around the circle.

Note: This exercise has group members getting physically very close to each other and helps build intimacy.

Variations:

- ☐ This exercise can also be done as a competition between teams.
- ☐ Use a piece of fruit, say an apple or an orange, instead of a balloon.

75 Win-Win

Purpose: To raise awareness of win-win solutions.
Materials: Watch.
Time: 10 minutes.

Process: Have participants pair up, standing facing one another. Have them take their partner's hand as though they are shaking hands. Say: *The object of this exercise is to see how many times you can put your partner's hand on your right hip in one minute.* Time one minute then stop the group. See what numbers people achieved and how they achieved it. Allow pairs to reflect on the way they interpreted this exercise. Bring the group back into a circle to share what they learned.

   Note: High numbers can be achieved if the pair cooperate— standing side by side and moving hands together from one hip to the other at a fast speed.

76 Team Names

Purpose: To generate a sense of team quickly.
Materials: None.
Time: 15-20 minutes.

Process: Form subgroups of four to six people. Ask each group to choose a name for itself, making sure it is secret from the other teams. Then ask each group to prepare and act out its name as a charade.

77 Effective Teams

Purpose: To identify what qualities make a team effective and to evaluate team effectiveness.

Materials: Paper and pens, whiteboard.

Time: 40-60 minutes.

Process: Brainstorm or list the qualities found in an effective team. Then have participants rank the top 10 of these qualities 1 to 10 (see Tool 10). Now have each participant rate the team on each of the 10 qualities. Use these ratings:

4 Outstanding
3 Good
2 Reasonable
1 Poor
0 Disaster ahead

Mark the results on the board. Identify the key areas the team wants to improve. Design a plan for each area which includes measurable results.

Note: If the team is larger than eight to ten, you may want to do the first part of this exercise in subgroups.

78 The Human Machine

Purpose: To encourage teamwork through nonverbal interaction.

Materials: None.

Time: 5 to 10 minutes.

Process: Have participants form groups of three to six. Ask one person in each group to start making a repetitive movement. Invite another person to join in with a related movement. Continue until each member of the group has joined in with a different movement. Suggested themes are:

- ☐ A washing machine
- ☐ A vehicle
- ☐ A monster
- ☐ A record player
- ☐ A device for peeling oranges

Note: This exercise, as with other physical exercises, can be useful during a long workshop or seminar when the energy of the group is low.

79 Treasure Hunt

Purpose: To encourage competition and speedy action.

Materials: A watch for each group and a list of treasures to find.

Time: Variable, perhaps 30 minutes

Process: Divide the group into teams of four or five people. Each group is given a list of treasures and a time in which to collect them. Each treasure found is allocated 10 points while getting back within the stated time is worth 30 points. Suggestions for treasures, which need to be different but comparable, for each group are:

Team One
- ☐ A tricycle
- ☐ A bird in a cage
- ☐ Something over 100 years old
- ☐ A Mercedes-Benz
- ☐ An unusual item of their choice

Team Two
- ☐ A horse
- ☐ A garden hose
- ☐ A flowering potted plant
- ☐ A hospital bed
- ☐ An unusual item of their choice

Team Three
- ☐ Five sticks of rhubarb
- ☐ An orange umbrella
- ☐ A bowl of custard
- ☐ A dinosaur
- ☐ An unusual item of their choice

One or two judges are appointed to decide the winning team. This may include the facilitator or preferably some innocent bystander who has been roped in for this purpose. When all the teams have arrived back, each presents its treasures and a winner is announced. Some creativity is allowed in distributing the points. The judges' decision is final.

80 Balloon Game

Purpose: A fun game for larger groups.

Materials: 4 balloons.

Time: 10 minutes.

Process: Form two teams of equal numbers in two lines facing one another about two yards apart. Give two balloons to each team. The object is for each team to throw the balloons over the heads of the other team—a goal. The team which scores the most goals wins. The facilitator is the referee and scorekeeper. The referee's decision is final.

P Tools for Resolving Conflict

All the Tools for Generating Ideas and Exploring Issues can also be used for working through conflict. Conflict resolution is more about clarifying the issues than working through opposing views. It is about coaxing out the issues and discovering where agreement already exists.

81 Using Rounds to Work Through Conflict

Purpose: To provide a clear framework and safe environment to work through conflict.

Materials: None.

Time: Most conflict-resolution exercises take time. Allow between 1 and 2 hours, depending on the size of the group. A minimum time for three rounds would be 6 minutes per person plus 15 minutes.

Process: Tool 2, Structured Rounds, is particularly effective for working through conflict as it provides a clear framework and a safe environment for expressing strong feelings. Encourage people to express their feelings and clarify the issues in the first round and then have a second and possibly third round to suggest solutions. Discourage participants from suggesting solutions before feelings have been expressed and really heard by other group members. Often being really heard is all that is needed. Quick-fix solutions can have the effect of covering over feelings, and group members who are upset will remain upset even though the solution is the agreed one. (The upset members will have collected new baggage and it is almost inevitable that this will affect the group later.)

In the second and third rounds, encourage people to develop their thinking each time and build on one another's thoughts (and not get stuck in a particular fixed position). The contribution of the non-triggered group members is important as they will see the conflict more objectively. Remember, the facilitator does not need to have a solution for the conflict—in fact it is better not to. Trust the group to work the issues through. Write up the issues and suggested solutions on the whiteboard as they are clarified so they can be seen by the whole group. When alternative solutions have been listed, have a round in which people state their preferences.

Note: What happens during this whole process is that the group expresses its hurt or upset, clarifies the issues, and finds a solution or course of action. It is the group working through the conflict. Your task as facilitator is to empower the group by providing a structure or framework for the group process.

Variation: Tool 1, Unstructured Rounds, can be used in a similar way for working through conflict.

82 Listening for Agreement

Purpose: To use the power of listening to hear agreement.
Materials: None.
Time: Variable.

Process: During a series of rounds (or during a free-flowing discussion) the facilitator listens for agreement and encourages group members to do the same. As the rounds continue, agreement will begin to emerge. Listen for this. There will come moments when agreement happens—when everyone aligns on a solution. A group member will speak the words, which express their own view, and this will also be the group agreement, as yet unspoken. This is the moment to listen for. Everyone will relax slightly, like a group *Aha—Yes that's it*. Alignment has occurred.

It can be heard by facilitators if they are listening carefully. Often it is so clear that it is as if a bell has been struck. This is the time for the facilitator (or group member) to intervene. Don't wait until the end of the round. Say: *I think we have agreement. Let's check it out.* Say what you hear as the agreement and ask the group for confirmation. If the group does not give confirmation continue the round (or discussion).

These moments are very important. If not captured, the group may move past the agreement and become unaligned again. Sometimes it is partial agreement that can be captured. *I think we all agree on . . . , can we confirm this? Now let's continue with a round on . . .* Using this technique, a number of partial agreements can be established which together lead to a group decision.

83 Fishing for Agreement

Purpose: To provide a process for resolving conflict where participants seem to be getting stuck in rigid positions.

Materials: None.

Time: 30 minutes.

Process: Have the key participants in the conflict sit facing one another in a small circle with the others seated in a larger circle around them. This is called *creating a fish bowl*. Have someone restate the purpose and values of the group, the results promised for the project and the time constraints. This will help to ground the exercise in reality.

Encourage the key players to speak directly to one another. Have each speak one at a time in such a way as to enroll the others in their own perspective. Have a time limit of about five minutes each. Allow a further two minutes per person for questions of clarification (not debate) from the other key players.

Then ask the key players to swap chairs or move one chair to the right (if there are more than two viewpoints) and speak from the perspective of the person who was sitting in that chair. Encourage them to really get into the role and argue passionately for the other's viewpoint.

Now ask the key players if anything has shifted for them. *What have you seen? Has your view changed and can you suggest a solution?*

Continue this process until each of the key players has spoken from every viewpoint. If there is still no solution, request the outer circle to make suggestions and proposals. If no solution emerges from that, ask the key players to meet as a subgroup after the meeting and come up with a proposal for the whole group to consider at its next session or meeting.

84 Bottomlining

Purpose: To provide a structure for resolving conflict which acknowledges and honors people's limits.

Materials: None.

Time: 30 minutes.

Process: After a round, discussion or fish bowl (Tool 83), when a solution has not yet emerged, ask each key player to nominate an unaligned partner from within the group (preferably with facilitation skills). Have him meet the partner and explore the key player's bottom line—that is, find out what is not negotiable in the issue as distinct from a nonessential preference or want.

Now have the unaligned partners meet and develop a solution which honors the bottom lines. The partners then check their solution with the key players. Ask the key players: *Can you accept this solution? Can you align with it although you are not getting everything you want?* Whether a solution has been found or not, bring the findings back to the whole group. The facilitator may like to ask the question: *What is the cost of reaching or not reaching agreement to the project and the group?*

85 Proposing and Counter-proposing

Purpose: To provide a structure for resolving conflict which concentrates on what can be done, rather than what can't.

Materials: None.

Time: 30 minutes.

Process: See also Discussion and action-planning, Chapter 8, page 71. The key players in the conflict and all of the group members are requested to keep proposing solutions until one comes up which people generally like the sound of—it will have a ring to it. Write it down for fine tuning. In particular, encourage the key players to continue proposing solutions and not get stuck in a particular position. Don't allow people to get into discussions about what won't work. Keep saying: *Propose a solution that will work. Keep going. Don't get stuck.*

86 Solution-storming

Purpose: To generate solutions using brainstorming.

Materials: Whiteboard.

Time: 10 minutes.

Process: This is a brainstorming exercise with all possible solutions being generated at speed and written up for closer scrutiny and analysis.

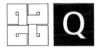 **Q** Tools for Ending and Evaluation

87 Action Prompts

Purpose: To create prompts for action at the end of a session or series.

Materials: Paper and small cards, 5 x 7 inches.

Time: 15 minutes.

Process: At the end of the session ask the following questions and have participants write down their responses on a sheet of paper:

- ☐ *What are the three actions you want to take within the next week/month?*
- ☐ *What cooperation do you need from others? (Be specific: what and from whom)*
- ☐ *What problems are you likely to encounter?*
- ☐ *How can these be reduced or overcome?*

Then ask them to take the small card and write down the three actions on it. Ask them to carry the card with them every day in their pocket or wallet.

88 Support Groups

Purpose: To provide an opportunity for participants to form support groups and buddy systems at the end of a group or series.

Materials: Paper, pen.

Time: 20 minutes.

Process: Ask people to write down the names of people in the group to whom they would like to offer support or assistance. Then write down the names of people from whom they could gain support or assistance (there will probably be an overlap). Allow five minutes. Give everyone time to make offers and requests, swap phone numbers and addresses. Suggest people make arrangements to meet or be in contact within one week. Allow 15 minutes.

89 Learning Contract

Purpose: To draw out the learning from a session.

Materials: Paper, pens, whiteboard (optional).

Time: 10-15 minutes.

Process: Ask participants to write down their responses to the following questions: (You may like to write them on a whiteboard.)

1. My learning from this session is . . .
2. I can use this to . . .
3. I will talk about this with . . .
4. I will increase my ability in this area by . . .

After participants have written down their responses, have them pair up and share what they have written with a partner. Then have everyone come back to the whole group and share.

90 Evaluating a Course or Workshop

Note: This is a general exercise for all kinds of groups. For groups which have been formed to fulfill a specific project, including formal project teams, a much more rigorous process will be needed. This will include evaluation of the specific objectives and measurable results developed at the beginning of the project.

Purpose: To have the group evaluate a course, or workshop.
Materials: Whiteboard.
Time: 30 minutes.

Process: Ask the group to reflect for a few minutes on the strengths and weaknesses of the group process and content and on the opportunities and learning that it provided. Then have a round in which participants share their reflections with the whole group. Write up the points on the whiteboard. When a point is repeated check the point already on the board. Encourage everyone to contribute and say what is there for them. If people say *It's already been said* encourage them to repeat it in their own words and add another check to the board.

This way everyone will get a real sense of what worked and what didn't work. Encourage a relaxed atmosphere in which it is okay to be frank. Participants may also like to acknowledge their own and one another's contributions during this time.

Variation: Use two rounds. The first looks at what didn't work and could be improved next time; the second looks at what worked and can be repeated. Always conclude with the positive.

After the round invite participants to rate the group or project on a scale of 1 to 10, with 10 being outstanding and 1 being dismal.

Have a quick round to get the scores. It is a good idea to get people to write down their score and swap it with their neighbor to avoid participants changing their score to conform with others.

91 Clearing and Completing with the Group

Note: This exercise is powerful as an ongoing process as well as essential when ending a group.

Purpose: To provide an occasion for group members to complete their involvement with a group, a group project or particular issue, and to ensure that no baggage is taken away from the group.

Materials: None.

Time: Up to 5 minutes per person.

Process: Ask each person in turn: *What do you need to say to complete your involvement with this group?* or *What do you need to say to be complete?* Then: *Is there anything else?* The person looks to see if they have any baggage to leave behind—anything that they would say to someone else after the group. Also what acknowledgments there are of themselves and others. The only response from those acknowledged is a simple *Thank you.*

R Advanced tools

These processes need a high level of group trust and skilled facilitation.

92 Self- and Peer Assessment

Purpose: To check out our own and other people's perceptions about ourselves and find out if there is any agreement. To gain insight into the nature of our perceptions of ourselves and others: *What basis do they have in reality? What is reality anyway?*

Materials: Tissues. Paper and pens are optional. These would be used to record comments made only if requested by the person in the hot seat. A recorder needs to be assigned as this must not be done by the person in the hot seat. Rotate the recorder as recording takes people away from being fully present to the group.

Time: This is a long process and takes between 30 minutes to an hour per participant for a group of eight to 12 people. Good for an all-day or all-night session.

Process: Have each participant in turn go through the following process:

Sit in the middle of the group or in an allocated hot seat within the circle. Ask the hot seat person to: *Share with the group all the negative perceptions you have about yourself, including your body, your personality, your intelligence, your creativity and spirituality. Don't hold back.*

As a round, the other participants now each in turn share their negative perceptions about the person in the hot seat. Tell the participants not to hold back. Being nice defeats the purpose of the exercise and is a disservice to the hot-seat person.

When this has been completed, call a silent one-minute stretch break before beginning the positive round. People should not leave the room or get involved in conversation. Now ask the hot-seat person to: *Share with the group all the positive perceptions you have about yourself, including your body, your personality, your intelligence, your creativity and spirituality. Don't hold back.* Next, the other participants share their positive perceptions about the person in the hot seat.

Tell the participants not to hold back. Encourage the hot-seat participant to really listen to and receive the feedback, particularly the positive comments. Invite them to take on board the feedback which is useful and let go of the comments which are not useful by *letting them go over your shoulder.*

Keep tissues handy as our culture does not provide many opportunities for acknowledgment and tears often come when people are being affirmed.

After the exercise is completed for every participant, have a debriefing session, encouraging people to share what they got out of it.

Note: After you have done this exercise a few times, you will begin to notice how we project our own negative and positive perceptions onto others. You will begin to realize that a person's feedback is revealing more about themselves than the person in the hot seat. Also the difference between so-called *negative* and *positive comments* becomes very unclear.

Variations:

- ☐ Self- and peer assessment can be of a general nature as above or focused on a specific issue or project. If on a specific project, the assessment would need to be against pre-agreed criteria such as the objectives and performance measures developed at the start of the project.
- ☐ Self- and peer assessment can be followed by self- and peer accreditation. For example, the purpose of the exercise may be to determine if a candidate is suitable for a job or project. After all the self- and peer assessment, a further round is held where each group member simply says whether or not they agree on the candidate's suitability for the project. After hearing this round, the candidate declares themselves suitable or unsuitable. If full agreement is not reached, the group may decline the candidate, or reconstitute the project.

93 On Hearing Bad News

Purpose: To allow group members to express initial reactions to specific bad news and setbacks which affect everyone in the group. This is for use in real situations, say when the group has a major disappointment like funding being declined.

Materials: Paper and pens for room-corner labels.

Time: Up to 1 hour, or more at your own discretion.

Process: The facilitator first introduces the stages of the grieving process which takes place when we hear bad news.

1. Shock, denial: *Oh no. It can't be true.*
2. Anger, blaming: *It's somebody's fault.*
3. Sadness, grief: *Poor me. It's not fair.*
4. Helplessness, fear: *What will become of me?*
5. Acceptance, transformation: *What's next?*
6. What opportunities are there?

Explain that all these reactions are normal and that the stages often, but not always, come in the above order. It is important to move through the stages without becoming stuck for too long in any one.

Then nominate a corner of the room for each of the first four stages (not acceptance, transformation because people in denial will often think they are in this stage). Participants are asked to move around the room silently for a few minutes exploring each corner. They may like to stand in different corners for a time with their eyes shut to get the feel of it. Participants are then asked to choose a corner which is the most similar to where they feel they are in the grieving process.

Participants then form into groups in the corners and share with that group how they are feeling. If there is only one participant in a corner the facilitator will need to spend some time with him or her.

After five to 10 minutes, depending on the size of the groups, call the participants back to the whole group. Invite them to share their feelings and concerns. Encourage participants to provide a safe environment for the expression of strong feelings. This includes being attentive and nonjudgmental. There is a tendency for people to want to physically comfort those in grief through hugging and cuddling. This can inhibit the grieving process and needs to be carefully monitored to see that it is useful to the griever and not an unconscious strategy by the comforter to lessen their own distress. If you are unsure, have the group provide physical comfort only at the spoken request of the griever.

Limits: This process is useful for expressing initial feelings. It requires skillful facilitation to move through the grieving process with people, particularly if group members have had little experience of personal development training. As the facilitator, be aware of your own levels of skills and experience.

Extension: If a longer period of time is available, say two to three hours, you can stop the whole group action at various points and repeat the exercise, giving people the opportunity to check out if they are ready to move to another corner—another stage of the grieving process. Always finish the exercise in the whole group with sufficient time for people to be ready to end the session and move on to other activities.

94 Body Love

Purpose: To appreciate our own and others' bodies.

Materials: Full-length mirror, tissues.

Time: 5-10 minutes per participant. Longer for the variations.

Process: Have one participant at a time stand in front of the mirror in front of the group and look at themselves in silence for two minutes. Then invite them to say what they appreciate about their own body. Encourage them to be specific: *I like my legs because they are strong and help me run easily. I like my hair because it is bouncy and curly.* Other group participants give free attention, but do not comment. Encourage each participant to keep finding more aspects of their body to appreciate, for at least five minutes. Do not allow participants to make negative comments or positive comments with a *but* added. If a participant becomes upset, encourage them gently to continue. This exercise can be very confronting for some people.

Variations:

☐ After a participant has appreciated his or her own body, other participants are invited to offer appreciation.

☐ Participants are invited to make negative comments about their body for, say, one minute, followed by positive comments for two minutes. After a participant has made the one minute of negative comments, the group is also invited to make negative comments for one minute. Then have the participant make positive comments about his or her body for two minutes followed by positive comments by the group for two minutes.

Note: Always complete each phase with positive comments. We are all highly critical of our own bodies. Our self-criticism is always more severe than anyone else's. This exercise starts the process of taking the heat or power out of our self-criticisms by sharing them with others and by hearing what other people really think about us. Keep some tissues handy as people often get upset.

95 Stretching Your Limits

Purpose: To identify what stops us doing what we want to do.
Materials: Paper and pens.
Time: 1 hour.

Process: Explain that we often feel frustrated by things we think we can't change. It is helpful to explore some of these situations to see whether they are, in fact, unchangeable. Ask each participant to think of something they would like to change. This could include starting doing something or stopping doing something or something in their life they would like to be different. Have them list all the things that prevent them from changing the situation. Then have them group these items under the following headings:

☐ *Hard and fast*—laws, physical impossibilities and specific directives from the boss.
☐ *Fairly firm*—company policy, cultural customs, standard organizational practices.
☐ *Flexible*—the way we usually do things or interact with one another.
☐ *Made-up*—a little bit of fact, but largely made up in our imagination.

Point out that some large organizations have discovered that 95 per cent of the constraints identified by supervisors could be classified as either *flexible* or *made-up*.

Have the group pair up and question each other's perceptions as to which headings various items have been put under. Have them choose one thing and develop an action plan to effect this. Come back to the whole group and ask the following questions:

☐ *What kinds of things would you like to change?*
☐ *What were some of the made-up things you would like to change?*
☐ *Give examples of action plans for overcoming limits.*

Variation: To provide a structure for supporting the proposed changes use one of: Tool 87, Action Prompts; Tool 88, Support Groups; Tool 89, Learning Contract.

Bibliography

Speaking and Listening

Butler, Pamela E. *Self-Assertion for Woman*. Revised Edition. San Francisco: Harper San Francisco, 1992.

Dickson, Anne. *A Woman in Your Own Right*. London: Quartet Books, 1982.

Lange, Arthur J., and Patricia Jakubowski. *Responsible Assertive Behavior*. Champaign, Illinois: Research Press, 1976.

Manthei, Marjorie. *Positively Me*. Auckland, New Zealand: Methuen, 1981.

Rituals

Beck, Renee, and Sydney Barbara Metrick. *The Art of Ritual: A Guide to Creating and Performing Your Own Rituals for Growth and Change*. Berkeley, California: Celestial Arts, 1990.

Starhawk. *Truth or Dare: Encounters with Power, Authority and Mystery*. San Francisco: Harper and Row, 1987.

Walker, Barbara G. *Women's Rituals: A Source Book*. San Francisco: Harper and Row, 1990.

Committees

Milligan, John. *Chairing Meetings*. Christchurch, New Zealand: Whitcoulls, 1985.

Mountjoy, Lora. *Effective Meetings: A Chairperson's Guide*. Wellington, New Zealand: Trade Union Education Authority, 1989.

Renton, N. E. *Guide to Meetings*. Sydney, Australia: The Law Book Company, 1991.

Teams

Adair, John. *Effective Team-building*. Aldershot, England: Gower, 1986.

Margerison, Charles and Dick McCann. *Team Management: Understanding How People Work Together*. Melbourne, Australia: The Business Library, 1991.

Group Resources

Coover, Virginia, Ellen Deacon, Charles Esser, Christopher Moore. *Resource Manual for a Living Revolution: A Handbook of Skills and Tools for Social Change Activists*. Philadelphia: New Society Publishers, 1985.

Doyle, Michael, and David Straus. *How to Make Meetings Work: The New Interaction Method*. Chicago: Playboy Press, 1977.

A Handbook of Structured Experiences for Human Relations Training. Edited by J. William Pfeiffer and John E. Jones. La Jolla, California: University Associates, 1974.

Hendricks, Gay, and Thomas B. Roberts. *The Second Centering Book: More Awareness Activities for Children, Parents and Teachers*. Englewood Cliffs, New Jersey: 1977.

Learning Peaceful Relationships: A Progression of Activities for Groups. Auckland, New Zealand: NZ section of the Women's International League for Peace and Freedom in cooperation with the NZ Foundation for Peace Studies, 1979.

Mariechild, Diane. *Mother Wit: A Feminist Guide to Psychic Development: Exercises for Healing, Growth, and Spiritual Awareness*. New York: The Crossing Press, 1981.

Men's Issues

Bly, Robert. *Iron John: A Book About Men*. Reading Massachusetts: Addison Wesley, 1990.

Keen, Sam. *Fire in the Belly: On Being a Man*. New York: Bantam Books, 1991.

General

Capra, Fritjof. *Uncommon Wisdom: Conversations with Remarkable People*. New York: Bantam, 1989.

Chatwin, Bruce. *The Songlines*. London: Picador, 1988.

A Course in Miracles. Tiburon, California: Foundation for Inner Peace, 1985.

Gawain, Shakti, with Laurel King. *Living in the Light: A Guide to Personal and Planetary Transformation*. Mill Valley, California: Whatever Publishing, 1986.

Hay, Louise L. *You Can Heal Your Life*. Santa Monica, California: Hay House, 1987.

James, Muriel, and Dorothy Jongeward. *Born to Win*. New York: Signet, 1971.

Kopp, Sheldon. *The Hanged Man*. London: Sheldon Press, 1981.

Prather, Hugh. *Notes to Myself: My Struggle to Become a Person*. New York: Bantam, 1976.

Tauroa, Hiwi and Pat. *Te Marae: A Guide to Customs and Protocol*. Auckland, New Zealand: Reed Books, 1986.

Zen Flesh, Zen Bones. Compiled by Paul Reps. London: Penguin, 1971.

Index

Bold type indicates major or defining references.
Italic type refers to exercises in the Toolkit.

A
Acknowledgment 19, 20, 26, 29, 40, 59, *141-144*
Agenda-setting **30**
Agenda-setting, open 30, **70-71,** *101*
Agenda, hidden 42
Agenda, open 30, 69
Anti-rambling device *127*
Attraction and repulsion **42-44**
Awareness 21-22, 34, **53,** 54, *124-125, 138*

B
Baggage **2-3,** 6, 14, 19, 29, 36, 42, 44, 48, 50, 51, 54, 56, 63, 65, 75, *118-123, 176, 185*
Being present b36-38, *124, 125, 134*
Beliefs 15, 17, 21, 36, 56, *121*
Brainstorming *92, 180*

C
Clarity **65,** 82
Collective or consensus decision-making **31-32,** 33, 58, 70, *101*
Commitment 5, 16, 18, 19, 26, **27,** 33, 49-51, 65, 77
Committees 32, 81, 83
Communication 21, 38, 65, *126-129*
Conflict 4, 18-19, 26, **44-48,** 50, 59, *175-180*
Continuum *96-97*

D
Decision-making 12, **31-33,** 45, 49, 58, 79, 81

E
Energizing *158-162*
Energy 5-6, 34, 41-42, 44, 49, 56, 61-64
Environment **67,** 74
Evaluation 20, *181-185*

F
Facilitator xi, 8-10, 18, 23, 30, 44, 47-48, **52-60,** 68-72, 76-78, 80-83, *154*
Feedback 59-60, **73,** 76, 78, 83, *104-105, 144*
Feelings 7, **13-15,** 23, 26, 41, 45-46, 50, *123, 138-140, 189-190*
Free attention *124-125*

G
Ground rules **28,** 45, 49-50, 58, 69, 75-76, 77
Group identity 4, 7, **15-16,** 19, 34, 80, *130-137*
Groups xi, 1-4, 9, **17-20,** 65

H
Humor 60, *158, 160, 167*

I
Identity check **43**
Individuals 2
Introductions *108, 109*

L
Large groups *82-83, 109*
Leadership **7-10,** 13, 15, 64, 80